Reversible
Quilts

Reversible

Quilts

Two at a Time

SHARON PEDERSON

Martingale™
& COMPANY

Acknowledgments

One person's name is on this book, but many people deserve credit—and my gratitude—for contributions major and minor. Going back to the beginning, thanks Mom (Mae Findlay) for teaching me to sew—and a million other things. Thanks also to Gail and Heather MacRae for more than you'll ever know; to Kathleen Shoemaker for years of friendship; to Dorothy Nylin for being my partner in crime; to Lynn McKitrick for supporting my latest whim and rescuing me over and over again; to Judie Hansen for bed and breakfasting, wonderful cartoons, and listening to me whine; to the rest of the members of the Lumbermen's Co-op: Ann Marie Potter, Joanne Corfield, Gladys Love, and Pippa Moore for inspiration and encouragement; to the members of ORQA, who keep me humble; to Jean Peters, who taught me the basic reversible block; to Kathleen Parton for having faith in me way back then; to Nancy Board for proofreading between the lines; to Lorraine Torrence for a firm kick in the butt; to Leland Palmer for not getting annoyed with his aunt when she forgot all the computer stuff; and last but not least, to my students who taught me just about everything I know.

Special thanks must go to Nancy Martin and the wonderful staff at Martingale & Company, particularly Ursula Reikes, Mary Green, Tina Cook, Stan Green, and Terry Martin. Thank you all for your patience and your persistence. It's been a wonderful experience.

Dedication

To Sy

A man of courage and integrity, patience and humor, love and understanding, whose love keeps me going.

Credits

President	Nancy J. Martin
CEO	Daniel J. Martin
Publisher	Jane Hamada
Editorial Director	Mary V. Green
Managing Editor	Tina Cook
Technical Editor	Ursula Reikes
Copy Editor	Liz McGehee
Design Director	Stan Green
Illustrator	Laurel Strand
Cover and Text Designer	Trina Stahl
Photographer	Brent Kane

Martingale™
& COMPANY

That Patchwork Place

That Patchwork Place® is an imprint of Martingale & Company™.

Reversible Quilts: Two at a Time
© 2002 by Sharon Pederson

Martingale & Company
20205 144th Avenue NE
Woodinville, WA 98072-8478 USA
www.martingale-pub.com

Printed in China
07 06 05   8 7

Library of Congress Cataloging-in-Publication Data
Pederson, Sharon
  Reversible quilts: two at a time / Sharon Pederson.
    p. cm.
  ISBN 1-56477-410-4
  1. Patchwork—Patterns. 2. Quilting—Patterns. I. Title.
  TT835 .P397 2002
  746. 46'041—dc21

                                    2002007528

Mission Statement

We are dedicated to providing quality products and service by working together to inspire creativity and to enrich the lives we touch.

Contents

I BECAME A QUILTER because of the *Oxford English Dictionary*. I had always wanted the complete Oxford, but I couldn't afford it. Then a book club offered it as an inducement to join, and I went for it. Knowing that I would probably forget to return the little cards prompting me to buy the next book, I decided to buy all four books needed to fulfill my contract and get it over with.

I chose nonfiction because reading hardcover novels in bed can be disruptive to your sleep. The darn things wake you up when you drop them. Since cooking was then my passion, I chose cookbooks, but they had only three I wanted. So for my fourth book, I chose a quilting book—an innocent decision that changed my life.

At the time, I was working full-time for a local politician. After being bitten by the quilting bug, I negotiated a four-day workweek. The following year, I negotiated a three-day workweek. But when I tried to get it down to two days, we decided that it was time to part company, and I became a full-time quilter.

My first quilting attempts were pretty funny, looking back from the perspective of fifteen years later. At the time, I thought they were amazing. I made very traditional patterns, avoided appliqué like the plague (because I couldn't figure out how to do it), and absolutely loved balanced, geometric designs. I still do.

At the time, I had over three hundred cookbooks, so my one little quilting book was pretty lonesome. I bought my second quilting book, which included Double Irish Chain quilts, and I was in love. I made three Double Irish Chain quilts, which made me the local expert, and was asked to teach it to our guild. I was terrified. After much encouragement, I agreed to do it, and I've never looked back.

Teaching quilting has been the most fulfilling job I have ever had. And Reversible Quilts: Two at a Time is my favorite class to teach. In every class, I hear students saying, "I just love this technique," and I love watching them light up when they recognize the potential of the technique.

I did not create this technique. It was created by an unknown quilter, who shared it with a friend, who shared it with another friend, and so on until it reached me. Now I would like to share it with you. I hope you have as much fun making reversible quilts as I have.

B EFORE YOU START, it's probably a good idea to read the following general directions ("Starting Out," pages 8–12, and "Reversible Blocks," pages 13–22) to gain an understanding of how the basic blocks are constructed and joined. Then you can learn about the many variations of the basic technique. After you have digested the how-to of reversible block construction, you can take the technique and apply it to any quilt you want. "Settings and Sashing," pages 23–31, "Borders," pages 32–33, and "Binding," pages 34–38, will familiarize you with all the steps necessary to complete any size quilt. Enjoy!

Side A of "Rae's Stars." See page 87 for side B.

Tools and Supplies

IN ALL OF my classes I give my "think like men" speech, which goes something like this:

Buy every tool you need to do the job. Buy only good-quality tools; you deserve them. And, buy every size of each tool. You can't do the job well if you don't have the right tools.

Your sewing life will be much happier if you have what you need to create all those beautiful quilts you have in your head. This is not an area of your life where you should be making do.

Rotary Cutter and Mat: I now have four sizes of cutters and find them all useful. But I love my 60mm rotary cutter for making reversible quilts. Remember, you will be cutting through many layers of fabric, plus the batting, so the bigger the blade, the cleaner your cut will be. Bigger is better with cutting mats as well. Buy the biggest one you can afford, or the biggest one that will fit on your work surface. Remember to store it flat and keep it away from heat sources. I found that packing it in a soft-sided suitcase in the back of a car with the sun shining on it was not a good thing.

Rulers: You'll need a square ruler that is at least as big as your block. I rarely make blocks bigger than 9", so my 12½" Omnigrid square is big enough. I also have a set of ⅛" clear acrylic squares that I bought from an industrial plastics store. They range in size from 3½" to 15½". With a permanent, fine-tipped marker, I drew one or more diagonal lines and added

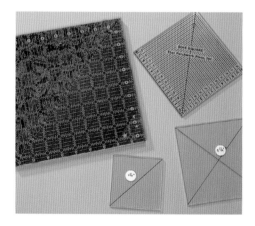

Purchased and homemade rulers

a label to identify the size. They are inexpensive and useful (see "Resources" on page 94).

Sewing Machine: All of the variations of the reversible quilt can be made on an ordinary domestic sewing machine. Treat your machine well, have it serviced at least once a year, and keep it clean and oiled. Lint sucks up oil at an alarming rate; it also clogs tension discs and bobbin cases. Clean your machine often and it will love you forever.

Sewing-Machine Needles: This is an area of sewing that seems to be shrouded in mystery and confusion. In every class, students ask "What size needle should I use for this project?" And my response is "What size thread are you using?"

There is a relationship between the thread size you are using and the needle. Sewing-machine needles have a groove down the front, which carries the thread as it goes through the fabric and into the bobbin. The thread should fit into that groove. The needle makes a hole in the fabric and the thread should fill that hole. If the hole isn't large enough for the thread to fit through, the seam may pucker. If the needle is too large and there is room for the thread to flutter as it passes back and forth through the needle, the thread may break. Therefore, it is extremely important to use the appropriate-size needle for each thread.

When selecting needles and threads, remember to buy only good-quality products. You are investing a lot of time in your project and you want it to last. Why risk damaging your quilt with cheap needles, or having it weakened by poor-quality thread?

It is recommended that you change your needle after eight hours of sewing. That's right, eight hours. I had one student say, "You mean, you can change the needle?" I was afraid to ask her how old her machine was.

Thread: Many years ago I received the following advice about thread:

- Match the fiber content of your thread to the fiber content of your fabric.
- Use the finest thread and the smallest needle that will do the job.
- Never use a thread that is stronger than the fiber of your fabric.

For basic hand and machine sewing, you need a medium-weight 100 percent–cotton thread. To tell the weight of the thread, look at the spool and you'll see numbers like 50/3, 60/2, etc. The first number

Needle Stickers

How do you remember what size needle you have in your machine? I buy small price stickers from the stationery store. When I put a needle in the machine, I write the size and type on the sticker and put it on my machine. If I use the needle for more than eight hours, I dispose of it. But if I use it for only a short time, I take it out of the machine, put the sticker on the blunt end of it, and put it in my pincushion.

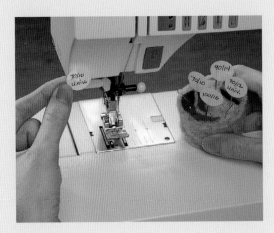

Using a Thread Chart

To make it easier to remember which threads are appropriate for which needles, I made myself a little chart. I bought four spools of cotton thread in the sizes I use most often (60/2, 50/3, 40/3, 30/3), and one spool of transparent nylon thread (size .004). I typed needle sizes at the top of the chart and thread sizes at the bottom. I cut a piece of thread from each spool and taped it to the appropriate spot on the chart, so now I know which size needle fits each of the five weights of thread.

This chart is also helpful when I switch to another fiber, such as metallic or rayon, where size numbers do not correspond to cotton sizes. All I do is compare the size of the metallic or rayon thread to the size of the cotton threads on the chart and I know what size needle to use.

The chart is only a starting point. For every project, particularly if I'm using a new thread, I do a test on a piece of the same fabric as my project. If an 80/12 needle is too small for that thread, even though it is the right size on the chart, I go up one needle size and see if I get better results.

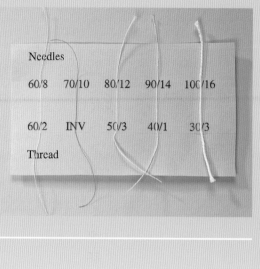

indicates the weight of the thread: the smaller the number, the thicker the thread. The second number indicates how many plies there are: the higher the number, the stronger the thread. That means that 50/3 is thicker and stronger than 60/2. I use 50/3 for all my basic hand and machine sewing.

My favorite color for sewing thread is medium gray. One of my first quilting teachers told me that if you use a thread that is lighter than your fabric, it will look like a picket fence across your quilt, whereas a darker thread will look like a shadow.

Walking Foot: Use a walking foot to help feed the layers through the machine evenly. This is especially important because you will be machine quilting without basting.

NOTE: *On some machines, it helps to reduce the pressure on the foot to avoid bunching as the* *three layers of the quilt pass under it. Check the manual for instructions and remember to return it to the normal setting when you are finished.*

Fabric

My favorite topic. For four years, I was a sales representative for a wholesale fabric distributor. My job was to sell fabric to quilt shops. My husband said it was divine retribution for all the years I bought fabric from them. Friends often asked me if it was like working in a candy shop and getting sick of candy. No, it definitely wasn't like that. It seemed that the more fabric I saw, the more I loved it. I anxiously awaited the arrival of the new swatches and I waxed poetic to my customers about them.

At the end of the season, the swatches were no longer current, so I was able to incorporate them into my stash. Given that my favorite quilts are scrappy, this is the perfect kind of stash for me. Every piece of fabric I acquired as a sales rep will find its way into one quilt or another. Well, that is, if I live to be two hundred.

You can use almost any fabric when making scrappy reversible quilts. In the "Christmas and Easter" quilt (page 40), I used every red, green, navy blue (and some purples) in my scrap basket for the Christmas side. In fact, there is only one true Christmas fabric in the whole quilt. And quite a few pieces are downright ugly.

I use only 100 percent–cotton fabric in my quilts, and I prewash everything before I put it into my stash. As with all other material, I use only good-quality fabrics. When I started quilting, I couldn't tell the difference between the good-quality fabrics and the cheaper ones. Foolishly, I bought some pretty cheap stuff and included it in a quilt. Not so many years later, the cheaper fabrics have faded, and the better-quality ones are still bright and colorful. But the whole quilt looks faded as a result of the cheaper fabrics. For the few extra dollars it will cost you at the outset, you will have many more years of use and beauty from your quilt if you buy good-quality fabrics.

The way to ensure you're getting good-quality fabric is to patronize your local independent quilt shop. They need your repeat business to survive and, therefore, will sell only good-quality merchandise. And, we need them to survive. Imagine your community without an independent quilt shop in it. It's a scary thought!

Care of the Scrap Basket

I live in a very damp climate. To keep a musty smell from developing in the bottom 12" of the scrap basket, I aerate my scraps on a regular basis. This, of course, allows me to dump the whole thing out and feel virtuous about it. Those of you in dryer climates will find an equally good excuse for this practice. While I'm wallowing in my mountain of scraps—fluffing them up and airing them—I feel like I'm seeing new-found fabric. Yes, I know I paid for it once, but when it comes out of the scrap basket, it feels like it's free.

And free is how you should feel when making your first reversible quilt. Let yourself go and use fabrics in ways that you haven't before. Use many patterns and textures together, or choose to break one of those rules (like not mixing stripes and plaids) that might have inhibited your quilt-making up to now. The quilt police are not watching you.

Batting

I USE HOBBS Heirloom cotton (80 percent cotton and 20 percent polyester) batting in almost all of my quilts. I like it because it has more loft than the other cotton or cotton-poly-blend battings. The polyester fibers are woven in with the cotton as opposed to forming a scrim, which means you can heavily quilt the batting (by hand or machine) without having it get stiff. A scrim is a thin layer of fabric similar to interfacing that adds strength to the batting. The recommended quilting distance for Heirloom cotton is 4". I presoak the batting and dry it in the dryer on low heat to get rid of the 3 to 5 percent shrinkage.

For quilts that are going to be minimally quilted, I use Hobbs Organic Cotton with Scrim. I like the fact that it is made of organic cotton. It is useful in situations where you want to leave lots of room between quilting lines. It can be quilted 8" to 10" apart. I preshrink it in the same way as the Hobbs Heirloom cotton.

I prefer not to use 100 percent–polyester battings for reversible quilts because they are a bit too slippery when I machine quilt without basting. Also, if I have two very different color schemes, one darker than the other, the darker fabric can show through a polyester batting to the lighter side of the quilt.

Design Wall

A DESIGN WALL is a vertical surface that you will use as a painter uses an easel. It is difficult to see how your design is developing on a horizontal surface. Half the fun with this technique is arranging and re-arranging the squares, so the larger your design wall, the better. In my studio, I have a wonderful design wall, which is 8 feet by 6 feet. It is made of a fiberboard (which is easy to push pins into) and is covered with polyester needlepunch. Cotton fabrics stick to the needlepunch, which makes it much easier to arrange and rearrange blocks until you get the perfect setting.

Try to get far enough away from the wall to focus on the value of the colors you are working with rather than the pattern on an individual piece of fabric. Often, when working at the machine, you see only the design in the fabrics rather than the value they will have when included in a quilt. To avoid nasty surprises, it is a good idea to put your reversible blocks on the design wall as you piece them.

I can see my design wall from the window over my kitchen sink. My studio was an addition to our house, which is why a win-dow that used to be on an exterior wall now looks into my studio. While I'm peeling potatoes or doing the dishes, I can look at whatever project is currently up on the wall, and from that distance, design flaws become obvious. I drop the potato peeler, dry my hands, and head for the wall to make the changes. Some nights it takes forever to get those potatoes peeled!

If it isn't physically possible to get far enough away from your wall, try looking through the wrong end of your binoculars or using your camera as a viewing lens. Both of them will accomplish the same thing, which is to reduce the blocks to the point where you can see only the value of the colors in the design.

In one quilt, I ignored my own advice and neglected to put the blocks up as I pieced them. It was a black-and-white quilt, and one fabric, which looked black on the sewing machine, read as a gray fabric when I got it up on the wall. By then, I had made about twelve blocks, and that fabric played a major role in all of them. I was dismayed when I saw it from a distance and had to remove the gray-looking fabric from all the blocks.

Now I realize that not everybody can have a wall permanently dedicated to quilt designing, but where there's a will, there's a way. With masking tape or push pins, attach white flannel or needlepunch to your largest available wall or the back of a door. This can be removed when necessary (a visit from the queen, etc.), but my guess is that it will be up more than it is down.

If you don't have an available wall or door, try using a room divider. You can often find them for sale in used office-furniture stores. Cover the fabric on the room divider with white flannel or needlepunch to make a portable design wall.

FOR YOUR FIRST reversible quilt, I strongly recommend making a scrap quilt. That way, you don't have to worry about running out of a fabric. If you use many different reds, then you don't need very much of any one of them, and you can always add another. It's the "magic porridge pot" type of quilt; there's always another fabric that will fit right in.

Pick your two favorite colors or your two favorite seasons, and choose fabrics appropriate to both. Don't worry if the two sides don't go together. With reversible binding, which you'll learn about later in the book, you can put pretty much anything you like on the two sides of a quilt.

Block Size

THE SIZE OF the block for a reversible quilt is entirely up to you. Having said that, I recommend working in block sizes that finish to 9" or less. Larger blocks are easily distorted when you machine quilt them without basting, which is how these blocks are put together. That doesn't mean you can't make them bigger. I have, but I prefer the results and the look of the smaller blocks.

Batting Squares

As I MENTIONED in the "Batting" section, I work with cotton or cotton-poly-blend battings only. Determine the finished size of your block and cut the batting square 1" larger. For example, if you want blocks that finish to 6", cut your batting squares to 7". This gives you the extra you need to square up the blocks later.

It is best to cut only two layers of batting at a time. The batting squares are your only reference point when you start, so they must be cut accurately.

Half-Square Triangles

THE BASIC BLOCK consists of a half-square triangle and a set of strips on each side of the block. For the triangles, cut squares first, and then cut the squares once diagonally to make half-square triangles. The size of this square will be ⅜" larger than the batting square. So, for a 6" finished square, cut the squares for the triangles 7⅜" x 7⅜".

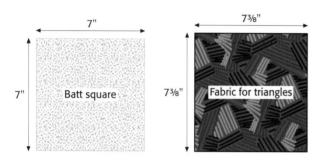

For your first reversible quilt, do not use directional fabrics for the triangles. Otherwise, the stripes in the triangles will be going horizontally and vertically. This wouldn't be a bad thing if that was what you wanted. But it is distressing to learn that

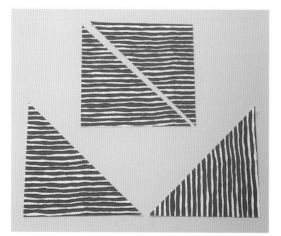

When cut into half-square triangles, directional fabric yields stripes that run in different directions.

you need to fussy-cut the stripes to get them going the way you want. This usually requires more fabric, and if you haven't taken this into consideration when you bought the stripe, you might not have enough.

Strip Cutting

STRIP SIZES ARE also entirely up to you. It is not necessary to match them with each other, nor do they have to be cut in ¼" increments. They can be any size you want. I prefer to cut strips between 1¼" and 2½", but those are just my preferences. If you are using strips from your scrap basket, pull them all out, no matter the size, as long as the colors fit into your proposed color schemes.

If you are cutting from yardage, cut one narrow, one medium, and one wide strip from each piece. That will give you plenty of variation. By narrow, I mean from 1¼" to 1⅜"; medium would be from 1½" to 1¾", and wide would be from 2" to 2½".

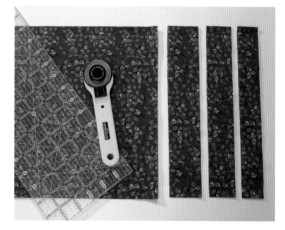

Cutting from yardage allows you to make strips of varying widths.

Block Assembly

Now you are ready to put your first block together. You should have a stack of batting squares in addition to triangles and strips for both sides of your quilt.

1. Thread your machine with 50/3 medium gray cotton thread and put an 80/12 Universal needle in your machine. For the bobbin, use a thread that looks good on the fabric you have chosen for the large triangles on side B of your block. When you sew strips on side A, the bobbin thread is quilting side B. If the sides are similar in color, you can probably use the same bobbin thread for both sides. If you have two very distinct color schemes, however, you will need to use two different bobbin threads, one to match side A and one to match side B.

2. Put the walking foot on your machine.

3. Starting with side A, place a large triangle, right side up, on a batting square so that the long side of the triangle (the hypotenuse) is ¼" beyond an imaginary diagonal line running from corner to corner.

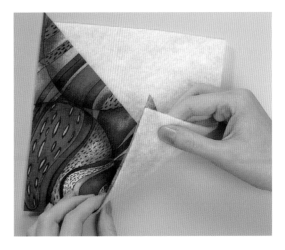

Check ¼" seam allowance by looking underneath batting square.

4. For the first strip, I recommend a wide strip rather than a narrow one. Often, while getting a perfect ¼" seam allowance on the side you are sewing on, you may get a wider seam allowance on the other side of the block. This is not a mistake. The extra seam allowance doesn't matter as long as the strip is wide enough to look good. Place the first strip on the edge of the triangle with right sides together. Make sure you can see at least one thread of the triangle fabric beneath your strip. This will ensure that the

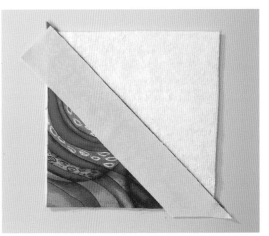

triangle doesn't slip beneath the strip (where you can't see it) and miss being caught in the seam.

5. Carefully turn the square over, making sure the triangle and strip don't move. Working on the opposite corner of the batting square on side B, place a large triangle and a wide strip just as you did on side A. The two triangles should be on opposite sides and opposite corners of the batting square.

6. Pin the strips and triangles on the stitching line. Normally, you pin at right angles to the stitching line, but for this technique, you place the pins *on* the stitching line. This will show you if you have an adequate seam allowance on the other side. Turn the block over and check. If the seam allowance isn't adequate, take the pins out and rearrange the pieces until you have at least ¼" on both sides.

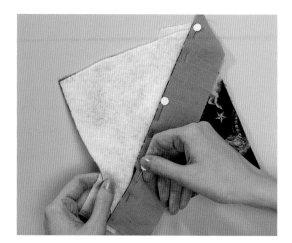

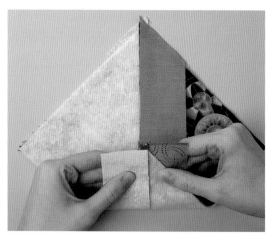

7. Sew through all layers using a scant ¼" seam allowance. If the seam allowance is wider than ¼" on the side you are sewing, it will be too narrow on the other side. This is the only time you need to use a scant seam allowance; you will sew all other strips with a standard ¼" seam allowance.

8. Open the strip and finger-press the seam; repeat for the other side. It is important to finger-press the corners well. If there is a little pleat near the corners, it will throw off the diagonal, which is what you will use later as a reference point to square up the block.

9. Up to this point, none of the thread is visible; it's enclosed in the seam on both sides. But as soon as you add the next strip, the bobbin thread will be visible on the other side. Make sure you have a compatible thread in your bobbin.

10. Choose the second strip for side A. It can be any width you want. Place it right sides together on the first strip, lining up the ends with the edge of the batting square, not with the ends of the first strip. Sew with a standard ¼" seam allowance. Open the strip and finger-press as you did with the first strip.

11. Continue adding strips until the batting square of side A is covered. When you are one strip from the end, choose a wide strip again. If the last strip is too narrow, there will be hardly anything left when the block is trimmed and joined with other blocks.

NOTE: *Don't worry if there's a little bit of batting showing after you add your last strip. You'll be trimming quite a bit off when you square up the block, and chances are, your little bit of "slip showing" will disappear then. If not, sew a small piece of fabric, trimmed off the last strip earlier, to cover the little corner of batting.*

12. Turn your block over and add strips on side B to cover the batting square. You'll be sewing on side B now, so make sure your bobbin thread is compatible with side A.

13. When you have both sides of the batting square covered with strips, it's time to square up the block by trimming the edges. Place your square on the cutting mat, with the diagonal seams facing right if you are right-handed or left if you are left-handed. With a see-through square ruler at least as big as your block, place the diagonal line of the ruler on the center diagonal seam between the triangle and the first strip.

14. With the 1" marks of the ruler in the upper right corner (upper left if you are left-handed), move the ruler until you come almost to the edge of the fabric on the right-hand side and the top of the block. Trim the side and then the top. You'll be trimming the minimum amount on these first two cuts so that if there's a problem when you turn the block over, you can do the first cuts over again.

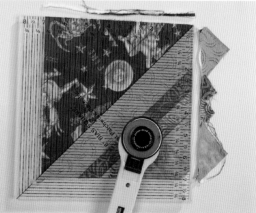

15. Now turn the block over so that the center diagonal seam is facing the same direction as the first side: right if you're right-handed and left if you're left-handed.

16. Place the diagonal line of the ruler on the center diagonal seam as you did for the first side. Keeping the diagonal line of the ruler on the center diagonal seam, move the ruler until the desired measurements on the ruler are on the previously cut edges. For example, if your blocks will be 6" finished, align the 6½" horizontal and vertical marks on the ruler with the cut edges; the extra ½" is for seam allowances. When you have the sides positioned at the appropriate measurements, trim the remaining edges of the block.

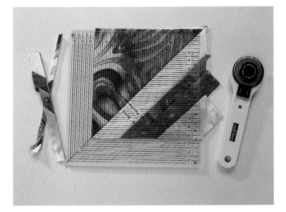

17. Place the blocks on your design wall as you complete them (see "Block Arrangement" on pages 24–25).

Block Variations

As you will see, there are many variations possible with the reversible quilt technique. Essentially, anything that can be joined with a sashing strip can be made as a reversible quilt. As long as you remember that whatever you sew on the second side will appear on the first side as the quilting lines, you can do just about anything you want. And of course, using transparent nylon thread in the bobbin often means that the quilting lines just disappear. The following variations are just the tip of the iceberg. I'm sure I'll go on making variations for the rest of my quilting life.

Block Variation 1

Use two triangles on one side. See side A of "Two Solitudes" (page 63). Instead of adding a strip onto the triangle, place another triangle on the first one with right sides together. Then turn the block over and treat the other side in any way you wish.

Block Variation 2

Use all strips on one side. See side B of "Two Solitudes" (page 64). Place two strips right sides together instead of one strip and a large triangle. Just remember to place the edges of the strips ¼" beyond the imaginary diagonal line running from corner to corner on the batting square.

Block Variation 3

Use two small triangles and one large triangle. See side B of "Hearts and Pinwheels" (page 47).

Block Variation 4

This one is the easiest variation. Simply place a piece of fabric the same size as the batting square on one side. See side B of "Two Solitudes" (page 64). Place the square of fabric, right side up, on the batting square and turn the block over. Depending on what you put on the other side, it may be necessary to add some quilting lines to anchor the batting.

Block Variation 5

When you use a prepieced or appliquéd block, you are, in effect, using Variation 4. See "Wild and Woolly" (page 72).

Troubleshooting

Unless you really enjoy ripping out stitches—or "reverse sewing" as my friend Dorothy calls it—read the following hints; they might help you avoid wearing out your seam ripper.

Obviously, if you have sewn on only one strip and you discover one of the following problems, you can tear it out and redo it. But, in some cases, there are alternatives.

A strip has shifted at one end.

Measure the narrowest part of the strip and cut the next strip exactly that wide. Align the strip with the stitching line, not the edge of the "slipped" strip. With a ¼"-wide seam allowance, sew in place, following the edge of the new strip. Open the strip and finger-press. Trim the excess seam allowance from the first strip if necessary.

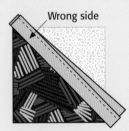

You forgot to open up the first strip on side B, and now it's caught in the stitching line.

With small, sharp scissors, cut as close to the stitching line as possible. Gently pull the remaining fabric from under the stitches. Nobody will ever know it happened, and you didn't have to rip out the side you just finished.

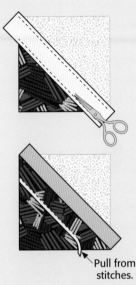

A center seam allowance starts out OK, but then disappears.

This is one situation where I recommend that you rip out the stitches. If you try to correct a seam allowance from the side where the problem is, you'll end up with two different diagonal seams. This doesn't sound too serious until you try to square up the block when you're finished. If you align the diagonal of the ruler on the stitching line on side A and do your first two cuts, when you turn the block over, the diagonal on side B will not be where it should be.

Not Only for Reversibles

WHEN IS A reversible quilt not a reversible quilt? I often use the reversible technique even when I intend to show only one side. Anyone who has machine quilted a queen-sized quilt knows that the bulk of the quilt is difficult to manipulate through that little opening in your machine. But if you break it down into smaller, manageable blocks, it becomes much easier.

When approaching a project, particularly one that will have a lot of machine quilting in it, consider making it a "reversible" quilt with plain fabric on the back. If you use the same fabric for blocks and sashing, you can make it look like a "whole-cloth" quilt.

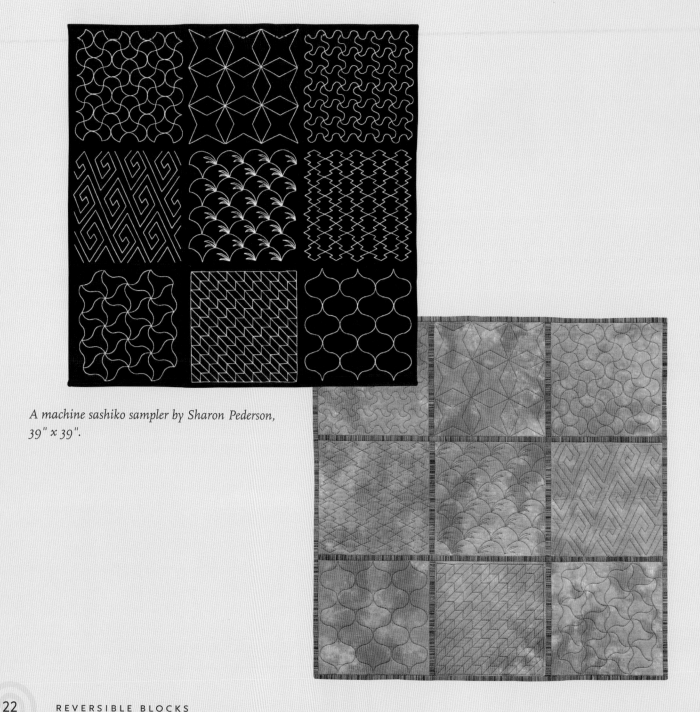

A machine sashiko sampler by Sharon Pederson, 39" x 39".

Ｈow often do you set your blocks the way you've always seen them done? If a pattern attracts you enough so that you want to make a quilt of your own, chances are that you'll set the blocks in the same way. The first reversible quilt I saw was a Sunshine and Shadows setting, so that's how I set the blocks in my first two or three reversible quilts. Then I decided to just make a bunch of scrappy blocks and play with them on the design wall. Either way is fun—starting with a setting in mind or just playing with the blocks.

When designing settings for a reversible quilt, remember that what you design for one side will be mirror-imaged on the other side. The examples below and on the following page show side A and side B for five common settings using the same block variation on each side. You can play with color and value, but the two sides look different. Notice that the direction of the diagonal stitching lines will be the same on both sides.

When you use a different block variation on side A and side B, you will not get a true mirror image as you do in the examples here, but the direction of the diagonal stitching lines will be the same.

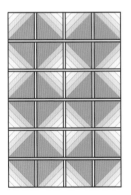

Sunshine and Shadow
Side A

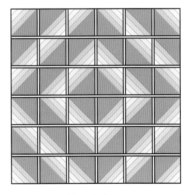

Barn Raising
Side A

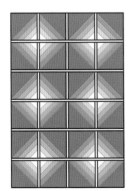

Sunshine and Shadow
Side B

Barn Raising
Side B

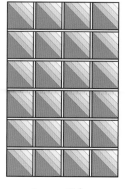

Roman Stripe
Side A

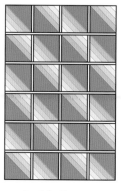

Straight Furrows
Side A

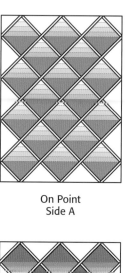

On Point
Side A

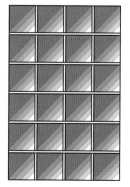

Roman Stripe
Side B

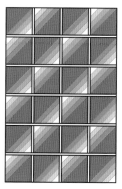

Straight Furrows
Side B

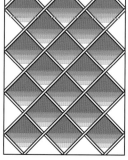

On Point
Side B

Block Arrangement

As you complete a block, arrange the blocks for side A on your design wall. Be sure to leave room above the first row of blocks so you can turn the blocks over and view side B. When you finish the arrangement for side A, that's only half the story. You need to look at the arrangement for side B to make sure it is what you expected. Number the blocks for side A in horizontal rows, starting with "1" in the upper left corner.

Follow the example on the facing page to see how the blocks for side A are turned over from side to side and repositioned for side B. Starting with the top row, turn block 4 over and move it to the first position of the first row. Then turn block 3 over and move it to the second position. Turn blocks 1 and 2 over to complete the first row. Repeat with all rows until you can see all of side B.

Now you can assess the colors and values on side B and decide if you want to make any changes in the block positions. Don't forget: changes you make to side B will also affect side A. After making whatever changes you think are necessary to side B, turn the blocks over as described above to look at side A once again. This is a process that can take hours, maybe days. I suggest you give yourself a deadline.

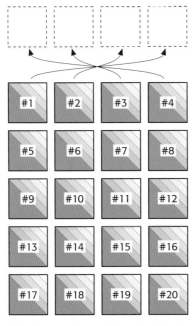

Blocks on design wall showing Side A

First row of Side B

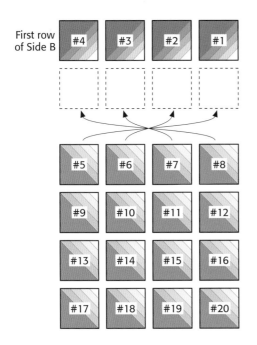

Sashing

SASHING, COMPOSED OF strips that join the blocks and rows, performs two tasks. It is not only the functional piece that joins the blocks, but it can also be a strong design element. Your choice of fabric for sashing can make a strong statement, as the red solid does on side A of "The Eleventh Hour" (page 77). Or it can make no statement, completely disappearing as you can see on the Pinwheel side of "Hearts and Pinwheels" (page 47). It can tone down a quilt that is a bit too busy. Or it can liven up a quilt that's leaning toward boring. The fabric you use for sashing can be the same throughout the quilt or can change from block to block; see side A of "Two Solitudes" (page 63).

Sashing Choices

When I am satisfied with the setting of the blocks on my design wall, I audition fabrics I think will work as sashing. If I have lots of a particular fabric, I don't mind wasting a small piece, so I cut a strip about ⅝" wide (which is how wide the finished sashing will be).

Cut strips from as many fabrics as you wish to audition. Lay the strips one at a time on the blocks to see how each one looks. Don't forget to stand as far back as you can to see the effect of the color on your quilt.

If you would rather not waste a piece of fabric, remove at least four blocks from the design wall, being careful to note their posi-

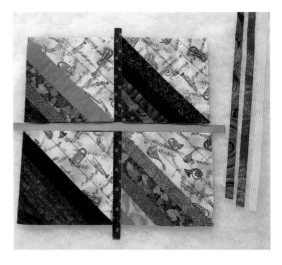

Using strips to audition sashing

tions. Place the potential sashing fabric on the wall. Then place the four blocks on the sashing fabric, with approximately 5/8" space between them. Keep auditioning fabrics until you find the one that looks best with the blocks.

Using a single piece of fabric to audition sashing

Don't forget that you must audition sashing fabrics for both sides of the quilt. Occasionally, one fabric will do for both sides (see "Christmas and Easter" on page 40), but more often than not, you'll need to pick two different fabrics.

Basic Sashing: 5/8" Wide

This is the method I was taught; it produces a 5/8"-wide sashing strip.

1. Cut strips 1⅛" wide from one sashing fabric, and 1¾" wide from the other sashing fabric. It doesn't matter on which side you use the two widths, unless you're doing a pieced sashing (see page 28). I usually cut the wider one from the fabric I like the least, or the fabric that was least expensive. Might as well use up more of it than a more expensive fabric I really love.

2. Fold the 1¾"-wide strips in half lengthwise, wrong sides together, and press.

To PREVENT BURNED fingertips when pressing the sashing strips, pin a piece of flannel to one end of the ironing board; this will protect the cover. From the back of the flannel, place a large safety pin so that the pin showing on the front side is the width your sashing piece will be when folded. Fold the sashing strip in half and push it under the safety pin. Pull about 6" of sashing through the pin and put the iron on the strip. Now pull the sashing strip through the pin and under the iron.

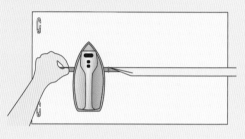

3. Use the full length of the strips. On side A, align the raw edges of the folded strip with the raw edges of the block. On side B, align the raw edges of the 1⅛"-wide strip with the raw edges of the block, right sides together. Sew *both* sashing strips to the first block with a ¼"-wide seam allowance.

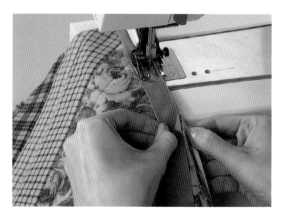

4. Trim the ends of the strips even with the top and bottom of the block.

5. Sew the second block to the raw edge of the 1⅛"-wide strip.

NOTE: *The edges of the two seam allowances should meet in the middle of the sashing strip and fill the space between the two blocks.*

If there is a gap between the two edges, increase your seam allowance; if the two edges overlap, decrease your seam allowance.

6. Continue sewing sashing strips between blocks until you finish the row. You now have three of the four edges of the sashing strips sewn by machine. Pin the folded strip in place, covering the machine stitching. Sew the remaining folded edge by hand or machine (see page 29 for machine stitching).

NOTE: *When I finish sewing a row of blocks together, I like to do the hand (or machine) sewing of the remaining folded edge before continuing with the next row.*

7. To join the rows or to add a border, follow the same directions as for joining block to block, except use longer sashing strips. If you need to join sashing strips, sew the ends together with a diagonal seam. Trim the excess fabric and press the seam open.

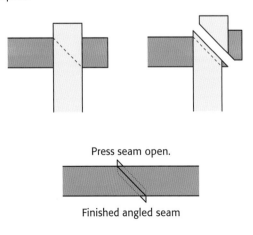

Press seam open.

Finished angled seam

8. When joining horizontal rows of blocks, line up the vertical strips between the blocks from one row to the next.

Pieced Sashing

On side A of "Two Solitudes" (page 63), I switched from beige to navy blue to orange sashing to maintain the illusion, created by color, of interlocking diamonds. To use only one sashing fabric would have destroyed the illusion. Remember, there are two sashings for each quilt, a single layer and a folded layer. I recommend using the single-layer sashing if you want a multifabric sashing—folded layers are too bulky at the seams.

For vertical sashings, sew different-colored strips between the blocks as described above. To use different colors in the horizontal sashing, you need to join the different colors before sewing the sashing to a row of blocks. In a perfect world, you would be able to precut strips to match the size of your blocks; for example, you would cut strips 8½" long if you are working with 8" finished blocks. However, this isn't a perfect world, and I don't know about your piecing, but mine isn't always perfect. So rather than precut the necessary pieces to

what I think they should be, I cut strips a little longer and join them one by one, measuring from block to block. While this may sound a little tedious, the results are worth it. Let's see how this is done for a navy blue block with white vertical sashing strips and white blocks on either side.

Measure the distance for the first piece of horizontal sashing, in this case white, and cut it a little longer. Then measure the navy blue block and cut a strip a little longer. Sew the white and blue strips together end to end. Pin the joined strips to the blocks, making sure the seam is aligned with the vertical seam between the blue and white fabrics. Now carefully smooth the blue fabric on top of the blue block and make a fold at the next seam between the blue and white fabrics. Finger-press the fold. Measure the next section for the white sashing and cut a piece a little longer. Sew the next white strip to the blue strip exactly on the fold. Press the seam open. Pin this portion of the sashing to the row of blocks. Continue in this manner, measuring, cutting, stitching, and pinning until you have completed the horizontal sashing for the row. Sew the sashing to the row of blocks.

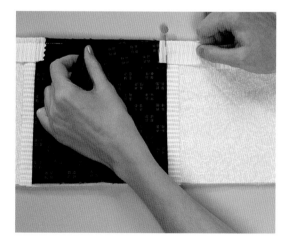

Align the seams of pieced sashing.

IF YOU CHOOSE to sew the remaining side of the sashing by machine, try the following methods.

Stitch in the Ditch

Pin the folded strip in place on side B. Sew from side A in the ditch along the seam of the sashing. Make sure the thread in the bobbin blends with side B; try using transparent nylon thread. Turn the block over occasionally as you're stitching to make sure the folded edge is caught in the stitching.

Side A

Side B

Narrow Zigzag Stitch

Pin the folded strip in place on side B. Sew from side B with a very narrow zigzag stitch. Use transparent nylon thread on both top and bottom for an almost invisible stitch.

Decorative Stitch

Pin the folded strip in place on side B. Sew from side B with a simple serpentine decorative stitch, with decorative threads on both top and bottom to match the fabrics.

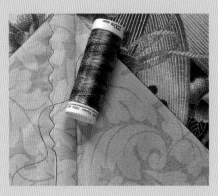

Side A

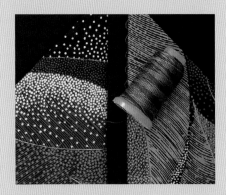

Side B

Wide Sashing

Some quilts call out for sashing that is wider than ⅝", such as "Geese Behind Bars," a detail of which is shown below. To make wider sashing, cut strips 2½" wide from both sashing fabrics. On the strips from one sashing fabric, turn one long edge under ¼" and press. Sew the unfolded raw edges of the strips to the raw edges of the front and back of the blocks.

Sew the next block to the strip that doesn't have the edge turned under. Measure the distance between the two seam allowances and cut a strip of batting that wide. Lay the batting in the space and hand stitch or machine stitch the folded edge down. To hold the batting in place, you will need to quilt the sashing strip.

Yardage for Sashing

The yardage requirements for sashing strips are provided with each quilt plan. But here's how to calculate the yardage if you're designing your own quilt. Let's say you're going to make 24 blocks, 9" finished (9½" including seam allowances). The quilt will be 4 blocks wide by 6 blocks long.

Side A
The strips for side A will be cut 1⅛" (which will finish to ⅝").

Vertical Sashing: You need 18 vertical sashing pieces, 9½" long and 1⅛" wide. It is not necessary to cut sashing strips to the actual length of the block. You will sew the entire strip to the block and then trim the ends.

42" ÷ 9½" = 4 (Divide 42" by the length of the block to determine how many segments you get from one strip; since you can't use partial segments, don't count fractions of a strip.)

18 ÷ 4 = 4.5 (Divide number of segments you need by number of segments per strip to determine how many strips you need. Round up to the next whole number.)

5 x 1⅛" = 5⅝" (Multiply number of strips times width of strips to determine fabric required for vertical sashing.)

Horizontal Sashing: For the horizontal sashing, you need 5 segments, 1⅛" wide and 38⅜" long. To determine the length of horizontal strips, add up the finished measurement of the blocks and the finished measurement of the strips, and then add a ½" seam allowance.

4 x 9" = 36"
3 x ⅝" = 1⅞"
36" + 1⅞" + ½" = 38⅜"

42" ÷ 38⅜" = 1 (Divide 42" by length of segments. It isn't necessary to actually cut segments to the measurement. You'll sew the entire strip to the row of blocks and trim the ends.)

5 x 1⅛" = 5⅝" (Multiply number of strips times width of strips to determine fabric required for horizontal sashing.)

Add the requirements for the vertical and horizontal sashing together for the total fabric to buy for side A sashing (5⅝" + 5⅝" = 11¼"). Round up to the nearest ⅛-yard increment and allow some extra for shrinkage and straightening the fabric. For this example, I would buy ⅜ yard of fabric for side A sashing.

Side B

The sashing strips for side B are cut 1¾" wide, so you'll need a bit more fabric. Since you'll need the same number of vertical and horizontal strips, you can simply substitute 1¾" for the 1⅛" used above.

Vertical Sashing: 5 x 1¾" = 8¾"

Horizontal Sashing: 5 x 1¾" = 8¾"

Add the requirements for vertical and horizontal sashing together for the total fabric to buy for side B sashing (8¾" + 8¾" = 17½"). Round up to the nearest ⅛-yard increment and allow some extra for shrinkage and straightening the fabric. I would buy ⅝ yard of fabric for side B sashing.

If you're using the same fabric for both sides, add the two numbers together before rounding up to the next ⅛-yard increment. Using the example above, 11¼" + 17½" = 28¾". Adding extra for shrinkage and straightening, I would buy 1 yard of fabric.

UITE A FEW reversible quilts don't have borders. In fact, the first four I made didn't. I started wondering why. Was it because it couldn't be done? Now that's a red flag before a bull if ever I saw one. If it couldn't be done, then we would have to find a way to do it, wouldn't we?

It didn't take a rocket scientist to figure out that you can add borders to the quilt in the same way you join blocks to each other: with sashing strips. Armed with that information, I proceeded to put a border on a reversible quilt. The first one I did was on "Hearts and Pinwheels" (page 46). It is a simple border with corner squares. I briefly thought of trying a mitered corner, but quickly discarded the idea. Given that you are usually trying to match a pattern on mitered corners, I decided that I wasn't going to try to do that and add a sashing strip at the same time. After all, this is supposed to be fun.

Basic Borders

DECIDE HOW WIDE you want your borders to be, and add 1" to allow for any slippage when quilting.

1.   Measure the width and length of your quilt through the center. Add an extra 1" in both directions to allow for slippage when quilting.

2.   Cut border strips for each side of the quilt according to your measurements. Cut strips of batting the same size.

3.   Pin or spray-baste the three layers together: side A border strip, batting, side B border strip.

4.   Quilt as desired.

5.   Trim to the desired length and width.

6.   Join border strips to the sides of the quilt with sashing strips. Then add the top and bottom border strips with sashing strips.

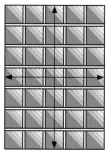

For borders, measure through center of quilt.

NOTE: *The sashing fabric used to join a border to a quilt can be the same as the border fabric or a contrasting fabric. It all depends on the look you want. If you use a contrasting fabric, the sashing will look like an inner border (see below, right).*

Borders with Corner Squares

FOR CORNER SQUARES, join borders to the top and bottom of the quilt with pieces of sashing. Then sew the corner squares and pieces of sashing to the ends of the remaining borders. Join the side borders to the quilt with sashing strips.

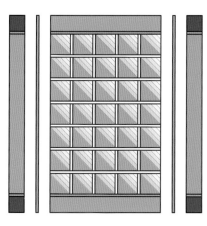

Borders with a Contrasting Inner Border

IN "GEESE BEHIND BARS" (page 67), you'll see that the sashing that joins the border to the quilt looks like an inner border. To do this, join the top and bottom border strips to the quilt, using contrasting fabric for the sashing. Referring to "Pieced Sashing" on page 28, sew a rectangle of border fabric to each end of a sashing strip for the sides. Sew the side border strips to the quilt with the pieced sashing strips.

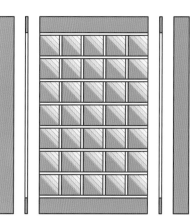

BINDING NEED NOT be just the "tidying up" bit at the end of making a quilt. Like sashing, it can play a decorative as well as a functional role. In some quilts, you may want the binding to just disappear, while in others you may want it to make a bold statement. If you are lucky, the same fabric will work on both sides. If so, use the "Basic Binding" instructions below.

Yardage requirements are provided with each quilt plan. To calculate the amount of fabric you need, measure the length and width of the quilt through the middle and multiply each of the two measurements by two. Add them together and then add another 4" for corners. For example, 42" x 2 = 84"; 54" x 2 = 108"; 84" + 108" + 4" = 196". Divide the total measurement by 42" to determine how many strips you need to go around the edge of the quilt: 196" ÷ 42" = 4.6667, or 5 strips. Multiply the resulting number times the cut width of the strip to determine how much fabric to buy: 5 x 2½" = 12½". Round up to the nearest ⅛-yard increment and add a little for shrinkage and straightening; I would probably buy ½ yard.

Basic Binding

REYNOLA PAKUSICH OF Bellingham, Washington, taught this technique to my friend Diane Beacham. Diane modified it a bit by starting at the corner instead of the middle of the side and taught it to me. I am forever grateful to both of them for creating such a great method for attaching bindings.

This binding is the same as I would use on a non-reversible quilt. From the width of the fabric, cut enough 2½"-wide strips to go around the quilt, plus 4" extra for corners. Join the strips end to end to make a long, continuous strip. Use the same technique to join them as for long sashing strips (see step 7 on page 27).

1. Fold the strip in half lengthwise, wrong sides together, and press.

2. Put the walking foot on your machine.

3. Starting at a corner and leaving a 2" tail, match the raw edges of the binding with the raw edges of the quilt. Beginning ¼" from the corner,

sew the binding to the first side of the quilt with a ¼"-wide seam allowance, stopping ¼" from the corner. Anchor your stitches at both ends.

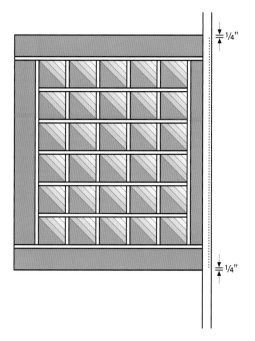

4. Remove the quilt from the machine. Draw a perpendicular line from the stitching line (A) to the fold (C). I call this the baseline.

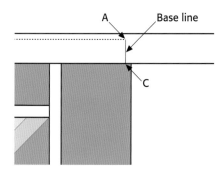

5. Measure the distance from the stitching line to the folded edge of your binding strip. It should be 1". Find the center of the baseline (it should be ½" from the folded edge and the stitching line) and make a mark. From that mark, measure ½" to the right of the baseline, and make another mark (B). Draw a line from points A and C to point B to form a triangle.

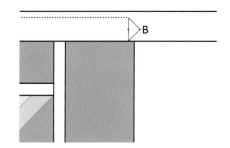

6. Fold the binding under at point B. Pin in place. If you can't see the triangle you've just drawn and the folded edges are not aligned, it's folded the wrong way. Starting with the needle at point A, anchor your stitches. Then sew to point B, pivot, and sew to point C; anchor your stitches. Do not sew across the baseline.

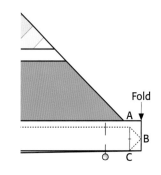

7. Remove the quilt from the machine and align the binding with the edge of the next side of the quilt. Mark the point at which you start stitching point D; this is under point A. With the needle at point D, anchor your stitches and then sew to ¼" from the next corner; anchor your stitches.

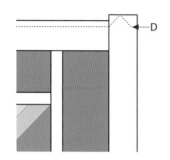

8. Repeat steps 4–7 for the second and third corners. On the fourth side, sew to where you started the first side (which is ¼" from the end of side 4); anchor your stitches. Draw the ABC triangle as you did for the previous three corners, but instead of folding the binding under, pin it to the "tail" you left at the beginning, aligning the folded edges.

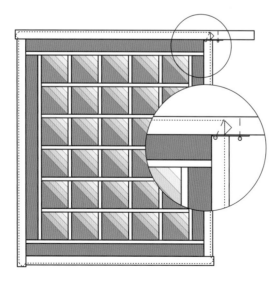

9. Sew the triangle through both pieces of binding, thereby enclosing the ends in the corner seam.

10. Trim the corners from each triangle and turn right side out. This gives you a mitered corner on both sides of your quilt.

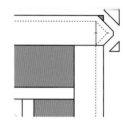

11. Turn the binding to the back side and hand or machine sew the folded edge to the quilt.

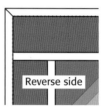

Reverse side

NOTE: *If you want to use strips wider than 2½" for your binding, the technique will still work. After folding and sewing the binding to the quilt, measure the distance between the stitching line and the folded edge (step 5) and divide the measurement in half. Use this measurement to mark the point of the triangle (B).*

Reversible Binding

BUT WHAT IF the same binding fabric just won't do for both sides of the quilt? My first encounter with the problem was "Two Solitudes" (page 63). With such different color schemes on both sides, neither side looked good with binding of the other color. In trying to solve the problem, I reinvented the wheel and invented a reversible binding, only to find out later that it has been done many times over by many quilters. At any rate, it meant that the two sides did not have to be compatible.

Reversible binding is easy to do, but you cannot do a mitered corner as you did for the basic binding. Instead, you will sew the binding to the sides first, and then to the top and bottom edges. Measure your quilt as described in "Binding" on page 34 to determine how much fabric you will need.

1. From the width of the fabric, cut enough 1⅛"-wide strips for each side of the quilt plus a few inches for the corners. Cut strips for the other side 1⅝" wide. It does not matter on which side you use the 2 widths; as an example, in these instructions the narrower strip will go on the front of the quilt. If the sides of the quilt are longer than 42", join the strips end to end as instructed in "Basic Binding," on page 34.

2. Fold the 1⅝"-wide strip in half lengthwise, wrong sides together, and press.

3. With right sides together and matching raw edges, sew the single layer of binding and the folded layer of binding together with a ¼"-wide seam allowance.

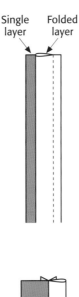

Single layer   Folded layer

4. Press the seam open. This helps the binding fold at the midpoint when you attach the binding to the quilt.

5. Sew the binding to opposite edges of the quilt first. With right sides together and raw edges matching, sew the single layer of binding to the front of the quilt. Trim the ends even with the quilt. Fold the binding at the seam line and hand or machine sew the folded edge to the back side of the quilt.

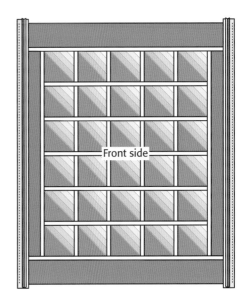

Front side

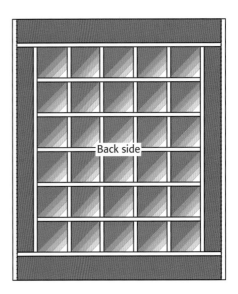

Back side

6. Leaving a ½" tail at the beginning and end, sew the binding to the remaining edges of the quilt.

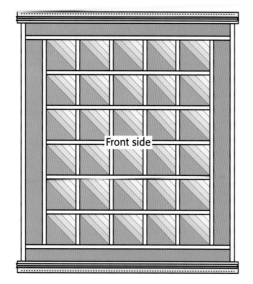

7. Fold the binding at the seam line, turn the tails under and whipstitch them by hand. Then hand or machine sew the folded edge to the back of the quilt as you did with the first two sides.

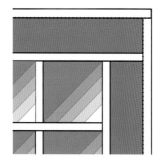

Labels

WHERE DO YOU put a label on a reversible quilt? Unless you can incorporate it into a block on one side of the quilt, I suggest you put it on the binding.

My sewing machine (and many others) has an embroidered alphabet, so I "typed" my name, where I live, and the current year into the memory. When I prepare my bindings, I sew this information onto the folded side before I sew the binding to the quilt.

MADE BY SHARON PEDERSON BLACK CREEK BC 2001

FABRIC REQUIREMENTS ARE based on 42" of usable fabric after preshrinking. In some cases, you might get 44", but I have assumed you won't. If you already have the fabric, check it to see how wide it really is, and adjust the cutting instructions if necessary.

It's difficult to provide yardage requirements for these quilts because so many of them use a variety of fabrics. When you see the phrase "total of assorted prints," it means that you need a combination of scraps, strips, and leftover pieces to total the amount given. If you want to use only one fabric in place of the assorted prints, simply purchase one fabric in the amount given.

Just in case there is someone out there who doesn't know what a fat quarter is, it is what you get when you cut a ½-yard piece of fabric (18" x 42") on the fold. The resulting pieces are each 18" x 21". This size lets you cut larger pieces than you could with the standard skinny ¼-yard strip of 9" x 42". When you are trying to increase the number of fabrics you have in a particular category—say reds or blues—without buying large amounts, fat quarters are a nice way to do it. Buying fat eighths is also a good way to increase the variety in your fabrics. A fat eighth is 9" x 21", the result of cutting a ¼-yard piece of fabric (9" x 42") on the fold.

Yardage amounts for sashing and bindings are provided for each quilt and are based on the cut width of the strips. For pieced sashings, you will need a variety of assorted prints to total the amount given. Remember, you will be cutting sashing strips for sides A and B in two different widths. The same is true for the binding if you are making a reversible binding. Since I don't know on which side you'll be using each width strip, I've provided the yardage amounts for each cut width. If you are using the same fabric for the sashing and binding and any other components in the quilt, add the yardages together and buy the total amount.

Projects

Christmas & Easter

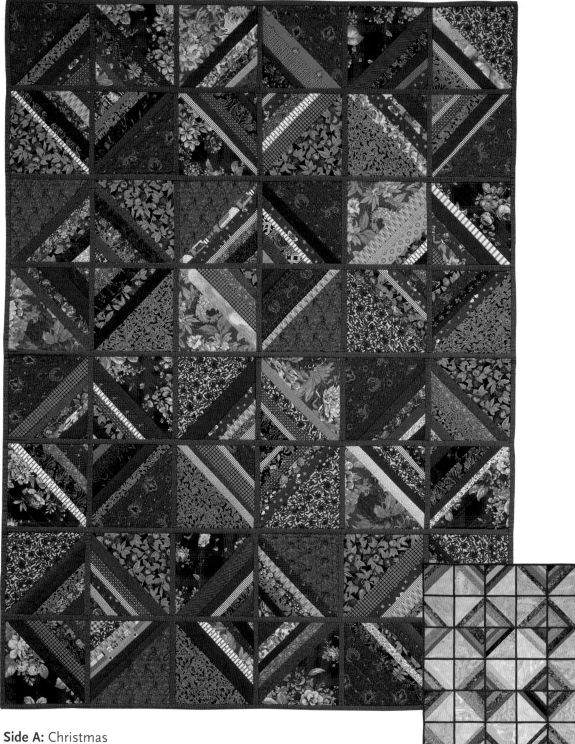

Side A: Christmas

57⅝" x 76⅞"; forty-eight 9" blocks set 6 across and 8 down;
⅝"-wide sashing. INSET: **Side B:** Easter

Materials *42"-wide fabric*

- ◎ 1¾ yds. 96"-wide batting
- ◎ 1⅞ yds. total assorted red, green, and navy blue prints for side A large triangles
- ◎ 1⅞ yds. total assorted red, green, navy blue, and purple prints for side A strips
- ◎ 1⅞ yds. total assorted green, pink, and mauve prints for side B large triangles
- ◎ 1⅞ yds. total assorted green, pink, and mauve prints for side B strips

For Basic ⅝"-Wide Sashing
- ◎ ¾ yd. for 1⅛"-wide cut strips
- ◎ 1⅛ yds. for 1¾"-wide cut strips

For Basic Binding
- ◎ ⅝ yd. for 2½"-wide cut strips

For Reversible Binding
- ◎ ⅓ yd. for 1⅛"-wide cut strips
- ◎ ⅜ yd. for 1⅝"-wide cut strips

Cutting

From the batting, cut:
- ◎ 48 squares, 10" x 10"

From the fabric for side A large triangles, cut:
- ◎ 24 squares, 10⅜" x 10⅜"; cut squares once diagonally to yield 48 triangles.

From the fabric for side A strips, cut:
- ◎ Narrow, medium, and wide strips as needed

From the fabric for side B large triangles, cut:
- ◎ 24 squares, 10⅜" x 10⅜"; cut squares once diagonally to yield 48 triangles.

From the fabric for side B strips, cut:
- ◎ Narrow, medium, and wide strips as needed

Side B: Easter

THIS WAS THE first reversible quilt I made. I emptied my scrap basket and pulled out every piece I thought would look good in a Christmas quilt. For me, that meant all the reds, greens, navy blues, and just for fun, the odd purple. There is only one Christmas fabric in the whole quilt, but to me it still says Christmas.

For side B, I also used scrap fabrics. I had taken a workshop that required many strips of different widths in two color families. I enjoyed the workshop but felt that I had the wrong fabric with me, so I just put the strips away. What do you do with a box of fabric strips cut into a variety of widths? This seemed like the perfect project, and so it became the Easter side of my quilt.

Even some of the batting came from my scrap basket. I was able to cut several squares from batting left over from previous projects.

Directions

1. Referring to "Reversible Blocks" on pages 13–22, make 48 blocks. Trim the blocks to 9½" x 9½".

2. Arrange the blocks for side A as shown in the color photo on page 40 or as desired. Referring to "Block Arrangement" on pages 24–25, turn the blocks over to view the blocks on side B.

3. Referring to "Basic Sashing: ⅝"-Wide" on pages 26–28, cut sashing strips for sides A and B. Join the blocks and rows with sashing strips.

4. Referring to "Basic Binding" or "Reversible Binding" on pages 34–38, cut strips and bind the edges of the quilt.

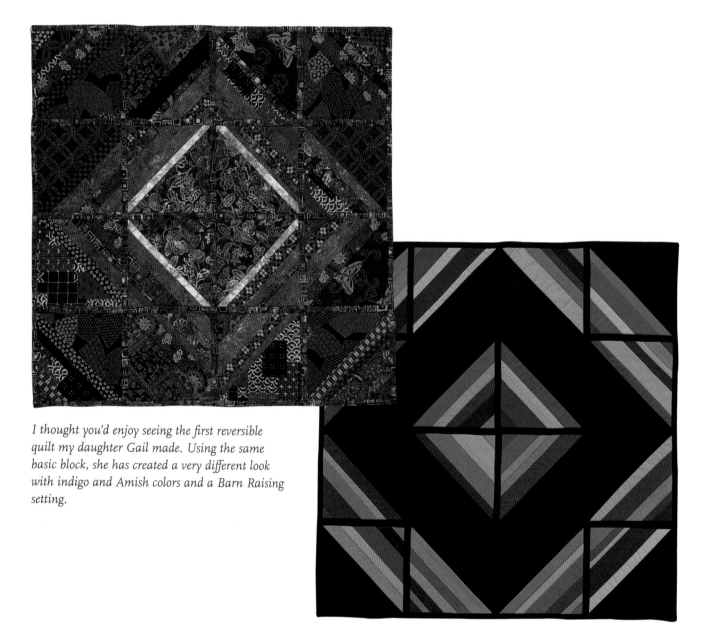

I thought you'd enjoy seeing the first reversible quilt my daughter Gail made. Using the same basic block, she has created a very different look with indigo and Amish colors and a Barn Raising setting.

Down Home

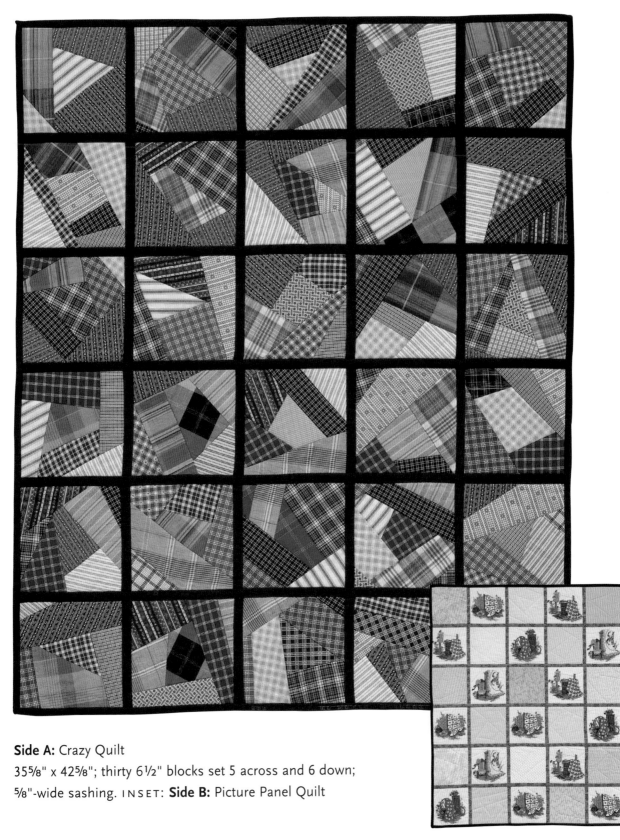

Side A: Crazy Quilt
35⅝" x 42⅝"; thirty 6½" blocks set 5 across and 6 down;
⅝"-wide sashing. INSET: **Side B:** Picture Panel Quilt

Side B: Picture Panel Quilt

Tʜɪs ᴡᴀs ᴛʜᴇ first variation of the reversible quilt I made. During a bout of insomnia, I lay in bed and wondered what else you could do with this technique. I had been given the little "picture panels" some time ago, and I thought this might be a good way to use them. And, of course, if it didn't work, I hadn't really lost much. For the Crazy Quilt side, you get to use those odd-shaped pieces in your scrap basket.

Materials *42"-wide fabric*

- ◎ ¾ yd. 96"-wide batting
- ◎ 1½ yds. total assorted plaids and stripes for side A Crazy patchwork
- ◎ 15 picture panel squares, 7½" x 7½", for side B
- ◎ ¾ yd. total assorted beige prints for side B

For Basic ⅝"-Wide Sashing
- ◎ ⅜ yd. for 1⅛"-wide cut strips
- ◎ ⅝ yd. for 1¾"-wide cut strips

For Basic Binding
- ◎ ⅓ yd. for 2½"-wide cut strips

For Reversible Binding
- ◎ ¼ yd. for 1⅛"-wide cut strips
- ◎ ¼ yd. for 1⅝"-wide cut strips

Cutting

From the batting, cut:
- ◎ 30 squares, 7½" x 7½"

From the assorted plaids and stripes for side A:
- ◎ See steps 2–6 below.

From the assorted beige prints for side B, cut:
- ◎ 15 squares, 7½" x 7½"

Directions

1. Place picture panel or beige-print square for side B right side down and cover with a batting square.

2. From one of the assorted plaids and stripes, cut an asymmetrical, 3- or 4-sided piece. Place it, right side up, in the middle of the batting square so that the sides of the piece are not parallel to the sides of the square **(fig. A)**.

Fig. A

3. From another plaid or stripe, cut a second asymmetrical piece. I like to cut them big and trim down. It's much easier than having to rip out a piece that's too small. Place the second piece, right sides together, on top of the first one so you can see just a little edge of the first piece; this lets you see how long your stitching line needs to be **(fig. B)**.

Fig. B

4. Put the walking foot on your machine. With neutral-color thread on top and transparent nylon in the bobbin, sew the 2 pieces together with a ¼"-wide seam allowance. Anchor your stitches at both ends of the stitching line. To anchor your stitches, set your stitch length to almost zero and sew about ⅜" of tiny stitches. You will be sewing through the batting and the block for the other side **(fig. B)**. Open and finger-press the seam. With scissors, trim the edges of the second piece so they are even with the first piece. With a rotary cutter and ruler, trim excess fabric that extends beyond the batting square, so the edges are straight **(fig. C)**.

5. Continue adding pieces until the square is covered. Make 30 blocks **(fig. D)**.

Fig. C

6. Trim blocks to 7" x 7".

7. Arrange the picture panels and beige-print squares for side B, referring to the color photo on the facing page. Referring to "Block Arrangement" on pages 24–25, turn the blocks over to view the blocks on side A.

8. Referring to "Basic Sashing: ⅝"-Wide" on pages 26–27, cut sashing strips for sides A and B. Join the blocks and rows with sashing.

9. Referring to "Basic Binding" or "Reversible Binding" on pages 34–38, cut strips and bind the edges of the quilt.

Fig. D

Hearts & Pinwheels

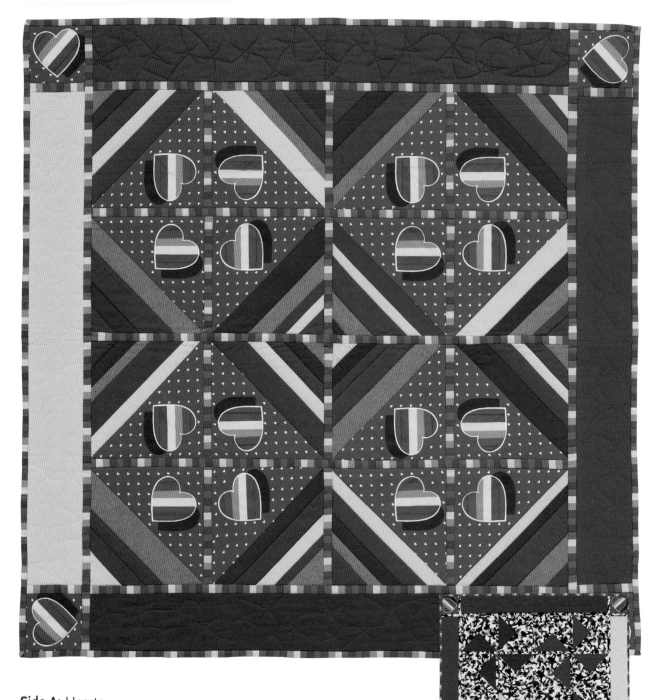

Side A: Hearts

$43\frac{5}{8}$" x $43\frac{5}{8}$"; sixteen 8" blocks set 4 across and 4 down; $\frac{5}{8}$"-wide sashing; 4"-wide border. INSET: **Side B:** Pinwheels

Materials *42"-wide fabric*

- ⊚ ⅞ yd. 96"-wide batting
- ⊚ ⅝ yd. each red, blue, green, and yellow solids for side B small triangles, side A strips, and sides A and B borders
- ⊚ ¾ yd. print for side A large triangles and sides A and B corner squares
- ⊚ 1 fat eighth orange solid for side A strips
- ⊚ 1 yd. print for side B large and small triangles
- ⊚ ⅓ yd. print for side A appliqué hearts (optional)

For Basic ⅝"-Wide Sashing
- ⊚ ⅜ yd. for 1⅛"-wide cut strips
- ⊚ ⅝ yd. for 1¾"-wide cut strips

For Basic Binding
- ⊚ ⅜ yd. for 2½"-wide cut strips

For Reversible Binding
- ⊚ ¼ yd. for 1⅛"-wide cut strips
- ⊚ ⅓ yd. for 1⅝"-wide cut strips

Cutting

From the batting, cut:
- ⊚ 16 squares, 9" x 9"
- ⊚ 4 strips, 5" x 36", for borders
- ⊚ 4 squares, 5" x 5", for corner squares

From *each* of the red, blue, green, and yellow solids, cut:
- ⊚ 1 square, 9¾" x 9¾" (4 total); cut squares twice diagonally to yield 4 small triangles in each color for side B.
- ⊚ 2 strips, 5" x 36" (8 total), for borders on sides A and B
- ⊚ Narrow, medium, and wide strips as needed for side A

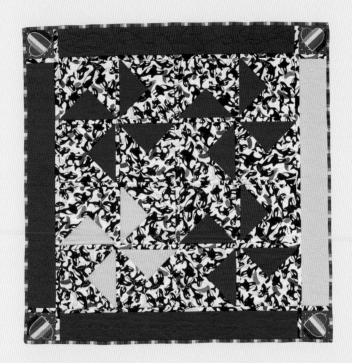

Side B: Pinwheels

I MADE THIS quilt for my first grandchild, Haley. She is now six years old and I still haven't given it to her. Don't drum me out of the Nana Corps yet; I did make her several other quilts. This one was just too good a class sample to give up. The hearts in the large triangles on side A were printed on the blue fabric. I fussy-cut the triangles so that the heart was centered.

From the print for side A large triangles and sides A and B corner squares, cut:

◉ 8 squares, 9⅜" x 9⅜"; cut squares once diagonally to yield 16 large triangles for side A.

◉ 8 squares, 5" x 5", for corner squares on sides A and B

From the orange solid, cut:

◉ Narrow, medium, and wide strips as needed for side A

From the print for side B large and small triangles, cut:

◉ 8 squares, 9⅜" x 9⅜"; cut squares once diagonally to yield 16 large triangles.

◉ 4 squares, 9¾" x 9¾"; cut squares twice diagonally to yield 16 small triangles.

OPTIONAL: *Use your favorite appliqué method to appliqué hearts onto side A triangles and 8 corner squares.*

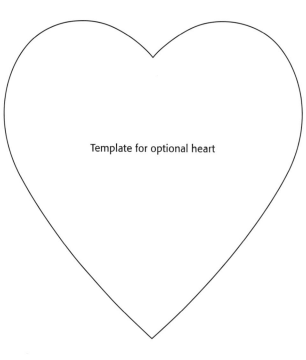

Template for optional heart

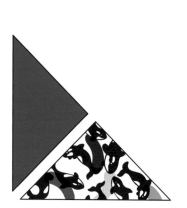

Fig. A

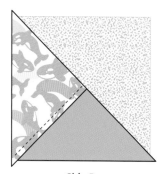

Side B

Fig. B

Directions

1.   For side B, sew each of the red, blue, green, and yellow small triangles to a small print triangle **(fig. A)**.

2.   Place a large-print triangle for side B, right side up, on a batting square. Place the pieced smaller triangles on top of the large triangle with right sides together **(fig. B)**.

3. Turn the block over. For side A, place a large triangle, right side up, on the corner that will be underneath the pieced small triangles on side B. Place the first strip along the edge of the large triangle with right sides together. Referring to "Reversible Blocks" on pages 13–22, sew the strips to side A **(fig. C)**.

4. Repeat to make 4 blocks for side B in each of the 4 solid colors: red, blue, green, and yellow. Trim the blocks to 8½" x 8½".

5. Arrange the blocks for side B, referring to the color photo on page 47. Referring to "Block Arrangement" on pages 24–25, turn the blocks over to view the blocks on side A.

6. Referring to "Basic Sashing: ⅝"-Wide" on pages 26–28, cut sashing strips for sides A and B. Join the blocks and rows with sashing strips.

7. Determine the arrangement of the border strips for each side of the quilt. Layer a strip of batting between 2 fabric border strips. Pin or spray-baste, and quilt as desired. Make 4 border strips. Trim the border strips to 4½" x 34⅜".

8. Layer 5" batting squares between 2 fabric corner squares. Pin or spray-baste, and quilt as desired. Make 4 corner squares. Trim the corner squares to 4½" x 4½".

9. Referring to "Borders with Corner Squares" on page 33, join the top and bottom border strips to the quilt with sashing strips. Join the corner squares to the ends of the remaining border strips with sashing strips. Join these to the quilt with sashing strips **(fig. D)**.

10. Referring to "Basic Binding" or "Reversible Binding" on pages 34–38, bind the edges of the quilt.

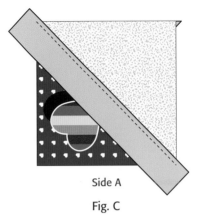

Side A

Fig. C

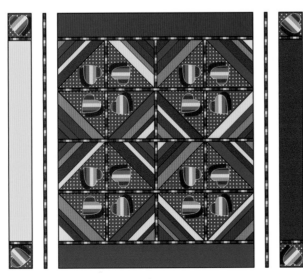

Fig. D

Down on the Farm

Side A: Red

43¼" x 43¼"; four 8" blocks; nine 4½" Nine Patch blocks, twelve
4½" x 8½" bars, ⅝"-wide sashing; 4¾"-wide pieced outer border.
INSET: **Side B:** Blue

Materials *42"-wide fabric*

- ⊚ ⅞ yd. 96"-wide batting
- ⊚ ⅞ yd. white stripe for side A center blocks and large triangles in border blocks
- ⊚ ½ yd. total assorted white prints for side A Nine Patch blocks and bars
- ⊚ 1¼ yds. total assorted red prints for side A Nine Patch blocks, bars, strips, and border blocks
- ⊚ ⅓ yd. blue solid for side B center blocks
- ⊚ ⅝ yd. blue print for side B large triangles in border blocks
- ⊚ 1⅛ yds. total assorted blue prints for side B Nine Patch blocks, bars, strips, and border blocks
- ⊚ ⅝ yd. total assorted white prints for side B Nine Patch blocks and bars

For Basic ⅝"-Wide Sashing

- ⊚ ⅝ yd. for 1⅛"-wide cut strips
- ⊚ ⅞ yd. for 1¾"-wide cut strips

For Basic Binding

- ⊚ ½ yd. for 2½"-wide cut strips

For Reversible Binding

- ⊚ ¼ yd. for 1⅛"-wide cut strips
- ⊚ ⅓ yd. for 1⅝"-wide cut strips

Cutting

From the batting, cut:

- ⊚ 4 squares, 9" x 9", for center blocks
- ⊚ 9 squares, 6" x 6", for Nine Patch blocks
- ⊚ 12 rectangles, 6" x 9", for bars
- ⊚ 28 squares, 5¾" x 5¾", for border blocks

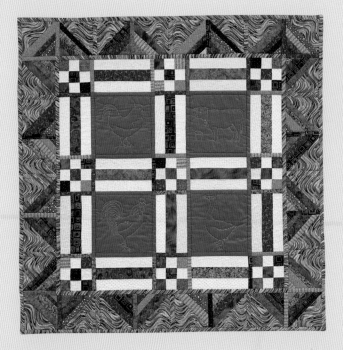

Side B: Blue

USING PATTERNS FROM *Redwork and Beyond* (Martingale & Company, 2000) I combined my two passions: reversible quilts and machine quilting. I also explored the use of the basic block as a border. The Nine Patch blocks on both sides required some alterations to the size of the pieces that make up the block.

To make this scrappy quilt, pull all of the reds and blues from your stash and cut pieces as you need them. If you run out of one fabric, you can always add another.

From the white stripe for side A center blocks and large triangles, cut:

- 4 squares, 9" x 9", for center blocks
- 14 squares, 6⅛" x 6⅛"; cut squares once diagonally to yield 28 large triangles for border blocks.

From the assorted white prints for side A Nine Patch blocks and bars, cut:

- 9 squares, 2" x 2", for center of Nine Patch blocks
- 36 squares, 2½" x 2½", for corners of Nine Patch blocks
- 12 strips, 2" x 9", for center of bars

From the assorted red prints for side A Nine Patch blocks, bars, strips, and border blocks, cut:

- 36 rectangles, 2" x 2½", for sides of Nine Patch blocks
- 24 strips, 2½" x 9", for edges of bars
- Narrow, medium, and wide strips as needed for border blocks. Cut strips 2" wide or less because blocks are small.

From the blue solid for side B center blocks, cut:

- 4 squares, 9" x 9"

From the blue print for side B large triangles, cut:

- 14 squares, 6⅛" x 6⅛"; cut squares once diagonally to yield 28 large triangles for border blocks

From the assorted blue prints for side B Nine Patch blocks, bars, strips, and border blocks, cut:

- 9 squares, 2" x 2", for center of Nine Patch blocks
- 36 squares, 2½" x 2½", for corners of Nine Patch blocks
- 12 strips, 2" x 9", for center of bars
- Narrow, medium, and wide strips as needed for border blocks. Cut strips 2" wide or less because blocks are small.

From the assorted white prints for side B Nine Patch blocks and bars, cut:

- 36 rectangles, 2" x 2½", for sides of Nine Patch blocks
- 24 strips, 2½" x 9", for edges of bars

Directions

1. Fold the 9" white squares in half twice to find the center of the square. Place the square on top of a pattern (pages 55–58), matching the centers. With a removable marking pen or pencil, trace the design onto the fabric. Test the marker before using to be sure the marks can be removed from the fabric. Repeat for the remaining 9" white squares and patterns.

2. Layer a 9" white square, a 9" batting square, and a 9" blue square. Pin or spray-baste.

3. Put the walking foot on your machine. With heavyweight red thread (I used YLI Jeanstitch) in a 90/14 Topstitch needle and 40/3 white thread in the bobbin, quilt the design **(fig. A)**. To finish the ends, pull both threads to one side, tie a square knot, and bury the ends between the layers.

Fig. A

◎ I found the designs easy enough to quilt with the walking foot. If you prefer to use free-motion quilting, put a free-motion foot on your machine and drop the feed dogs.

◎ You can also hand stitch the designs with a backstitch. However, the thread color will be the same on both sides; the advantage to machine quilting is you get to choose two different colors of thread.

4. Centering the design, trim the blocks to 8½" x 8½".

5. Sew the pieces for the Nine Patch blocks together as shown. Make 9 red Nine Patch blocks for side A **(fig. B)** and 9 blue Nine Patch blocks for side B **(fig. C)**.

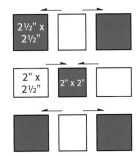

Make 9 red
for Side A.

Fig. B

6. Layer a red Nine Patch block, a 6" batting square, and a blue Nine Patch block. To align the blocks, put a straight pin through the corner of the center square and line it up with the corresponding corner of the center square underneath. Holding the block up so you can see both sides, continue aligning and pinning seam lines around the outside edges **(fig. D)**.

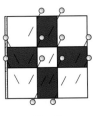

Fig. D

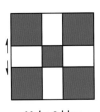

Make 9 blue
for Side B.

Fig. C

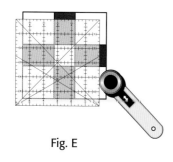

Fig. E

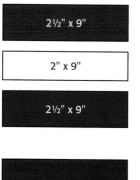

2½" x 9"

2" x 9"

2½" x 9"

Make 12 red for side A.

Fig. F

2½" x 9"

2" x 9"

2½" x 9"

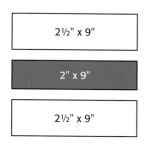

Make 12 blue for side B.

Fig. G

7. Quilt as desired. I stipple-quilted the four light-colored squares from the blue side with off-white thread in the needle and transparent nylon thread in the bobbin.

8. Trim the Nine Patch blocks to 5" x 5". To do this, measure 1¾" from the edge of the center square and trim; then turn the block and do the same on the other 3 sides **(fig. E)**.

9. To make the bars for side A, sew a 2½" x 9" red strip to opposite sides of a 2" x 9" white strip **(fig. F)**. Make 12 bars. For side B, sew a 2½" x 9" white strip to opposite sides of a 2" x 9" blue strip **(fig. G)**. Make 12 bars.

10. Layer a red bar, a 6" x 9" batting rectangle, and a blue bar. Align and pin the seams as you did for the Nine Patch blocks. Quilt as desired.

11. Trim the bars to 5" x 8½". To do this, measure 1¾" from the edge of the center strip and trim. Turn the bar around to trim the other side.

12. Arrange the center squares, Nine Patch blocks, and bars for side A **(fig. H)**. Referring to "Block Arrangement" on pages 24–25, turn the blocks over to view the blocks on side B.

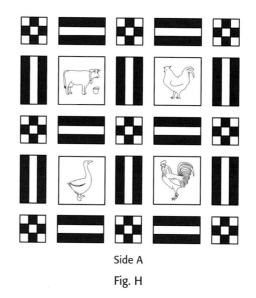

Side A

Fig. H

13. Referring to "Basic Sashing: ⅝"-Wide" on pages 26–28, cut sashing strips for sides A and B. Sew the units together in horizontal rows with sashing strips. Referring to "Pieced Sashing" on pages 28–30, sew the rows together with pieced sashing strips.

14. Referring to "Reversible Blocks" on pages 13–22, make 28 blocks for the outer border. Use the twenty-eight 5¾" batting squares and large white triangles for side A and large blue triangles for side B. Trim the blocks to 5¼" x 5¼".

15. Referring to "Basic Sashing: ⅝"-Wide" on pages 26–27, cut sashing strips for sides A and B. Sew 6 border blocks together with sashing strips to make each of the top and bottom border strips **(fig. I)**. Sew 8 border blocks together with sashing strips to make each of the side border strips **(fig. J)**.

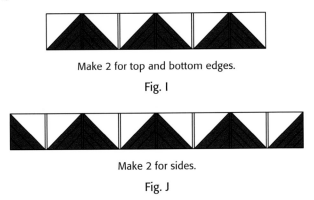

Make 2 for top and bottom edges.

Fig. I

Make 2 for sides.

Fig. J

16. Referring to "Basic Borders" on page 32, sew the top and bottom border strips to the quilt with sashing strips. Sew the side border strips to the quilt with sashing strips.

17. Referring to "Basic Binding" or "Reversible Binding" on pages 34–38, bind the edges of the quilt.

CBC Stereo

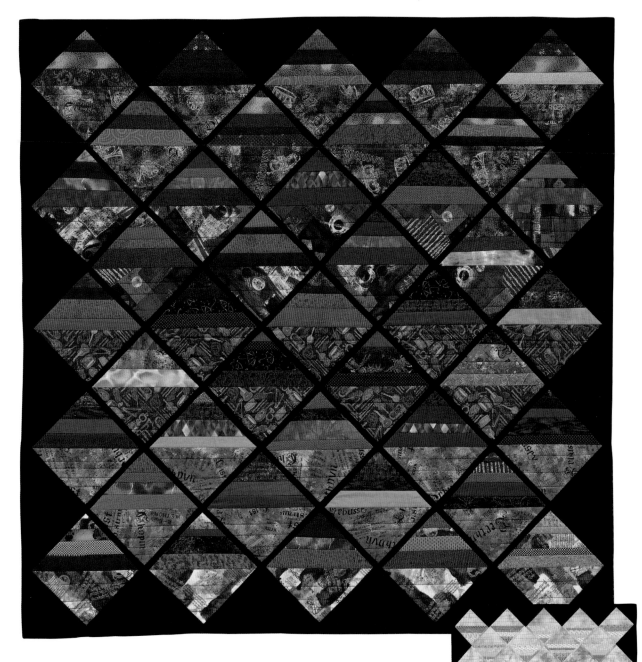

Side A: Music and Drama

62³⁄₈" x 62³⁄₈"; forty-one 8" blocks set on point; ⁵⁄₈"-wide sashing.

I N S E T: **Side B:** News and Weather

Side B: News and Weather

Iᴎ ᴍʏ sᴛᴜᴅɪᴏ I listen to CBC Radio Two, as it is now known, but when I made this quilt, it was referred to as CBC Stereo. It is the classical music network of Canada's public radio system. The programming is mostly classical music, with a little bit of drama, and most important, there are no commercials. There are occasional interruptions for the news and weather and a bit of sports news.

Side A, this quilt's colorful side, is made up of musical fabrics. Some have instruments, some include composers' names, and some feature musical notations. I think that side represents Radio Two's music and drama, while the other side, made up of grays, represents the news and the weather. Living, as I do, on Canada's West Coast, I'm used to gray skies.

To achieve the rows of color on side A and the gradation of colors on side B, you will have to plan the fabric placement for this quilt carefully.

Materials *42"-wide fabric*

- ◎ 1¾ yds. 96"-wide batting
- ◎ 1½ yds. black fabric for sides A and B side and corner triangles
- ◎ 1⅔ yds. total assorted prints for side A large triangles
- ◎ 2 yds. total assorted prints for side A strips
- ◎ 1⅔ yds. total hand-dyed gray fabrics in 6 gradations for side B large triangles
- ◎ 2 yds. total assorted white, gray, and black prints for side B strips

For Basic ⅝"-Wide Sashing
- ◎ 1 yd. for 1⅛"-wide cut strips
- ◎ 1⅓ yds. for 1¾"-wide cut strips

For Basic Binding
- ◎ ⅝ yd. for 2½"-wide cut strips

For Reversible Binding
- ◎ ⅓ yd. for 1⅛"-wide cut strips
- ◎ ⅜ yd. for 1⅝"-wide cut strips

Cutting

From the batting, cut:
- ◎ 41 squares, 9" x 9"
- ◎ 4 squares, 14" x 14"; cut squares twice diagonally to yield 16 side triangles.
- ◎ 2 squares, 8" x 8"; cut squares once diagonally to yield 4 corner triangles.

From the black fabric for side and corner triangles, cut:
- ◎ 8 squares, 14" x 14"; cut squares twice diagonally to yield 32 side triangles for sides A and B.
- ◎ 4 squares, 8" x 8"; cut squares once diagonally to yield 8 corner triangles for sides A and B.

From the assorted prints for side A large triangles, cut:

- 21 squares, 9⅜" x 9⅜"; cut squares once diagonally to yield 42 large triangles (you will use only 41).

From the assorted prints for side A strips, cut:

- Narrow, medium, and wide strips as needed

From the assorted hand-dyed gray fabrics for side B large triangles, cut:

- 21 squares, 9⅜" x 9⅜"; cut squares once diagonally to yield 42 large triangles (you will use only 41).

From the assorted white, gray, and black prints for side B strips, cut:

- Narrow, medium, and wide strips as needed

Directions

1. Make a colored sketch for each side. Starting in the upper left for side A and the upper right for side B, number the blocks from 1 to 41.

2. Referring to your colored sketches and "Reversible Blocks" on pages 13–22, make 41 blocks. Trim the blocks to 8½" x 8½".

3. Referring to your colored sketch, arrange the blocks for side A in diagonal rows. Referring to "Block Arrangement" on pages 24–25, turn the blocks over to view the blocks on side B **(fig. A)**.

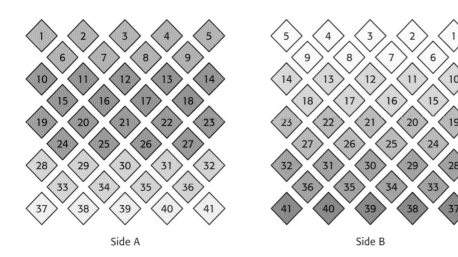

Side A   Side B

Fig. A

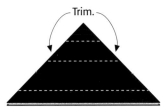

Trim.

Side setting triangle

Fig. B

Corner setting triangle

Trim.

Fig. C

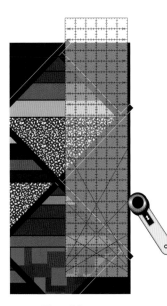

Trim 1" from
points of blocks.

Fig. D

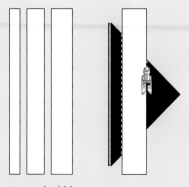

To quilt straight lines on the triangles without having to draw quilting lines, use different widths of paper as stitching guides. Cut several different widths, from 1¼" to 2". Place a guide next to a stitching line and sew along the opposite edge. The result will look like the quilting on the rest of the blocks.

Assorted-width
paper strips

4. Place a batting triangle between 2 black triangles. Pin or spray-baste; quilt as desired. Repeat for all side and corner triangles.

5. Straighten the edges of the 2 short sides of the side triangles, trimming the minimum amount; leave the long side as is for now (**fig. B**). Straighten the edge of the long side of the corner triangles, trimming the minimum amount; leave the 2 short sides as is for now (**fig. C**).

6. Add the side and corner triangles to the diagonal rows of blocks.

7. Referring to "Basic Sashing: ⅝"-Wide" on pages 26–28 for side A, and "Pieced Sashing" on pages 28–30 for side B, cut sashing strips for sides A and B. Join the blocks and triangles in diagonal rows with sashing strips. Then join the rows with sashing strips.

8. To straighten the edges of the quilt, place the 1" mark of a long ruler on the points of the blocks and trim along the edge of the ruler with a rotary cutter (**fig. D**).

9. Referring to "Basic Binding" or "Reversible Binding" on pages 34–38, bind the edges of the quilt.

Two Solitudes

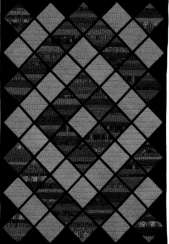

Side A: Interlocking Diamonds
48¼" x 67"; fifty-nine 6" blocks set on point; ⅝"-wide sashing.
INSET: **Side B:** Red Barn Raising

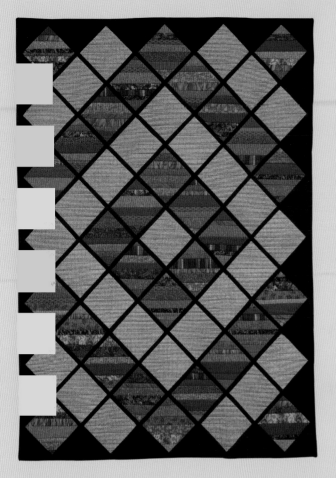

Side B: Red Barn Raising

Τ HIS WAS THE first reversible quilt I made with a controlled pattern on each side. I had been hoarding the Japanese indigo prints and the Indonesian batiks for a long time and finally felt that this was the right quilt in which to use them. For the red side B, I cut three strips from every red in my stash: a narrow, a medium, and a wide strip. It could be done with fewer reds, but my feeling is the more variety, the better.

Materials *42"-wide fabric*

- ◎ 1⅜ yds. 96"-wide batting
- ◎ ¾ yd. total assorted Japanese indigo prints for side A blocks
- ◎ ¾ yd. total assorted Indonesian batiks for side A blocks
- ◎ 2 yds. total assorted tone-on-tone beige prints for side A blocks
- ◎ 1⅛ yds. red print for side B plain blocks
- ◎ 1½ yds. total assorted red prints for side B strips
- ◎ ¾ yd. black solid for side B side and corner triangles

For Basic ⅝"-Wide Sashing
- ◎ ⅞ yd. for 1⅛"-wide cut strips
- ◎ 1⅓ yds. for 1¾"-wide cut strips

For Basic Binding
- ◎ ½ yd. for 2½"-wide cut strips

For Reversible Binding
- ◎ ¼ yd. for 1⅛"-wide cut strips
- ◎ ⅜ yd. for 1⅝"-wide cut strips

Cutting

From the batting, cut:
- ◎ 59 squares, 7" x 7", for blocks
- ◎ 5 squares, 11" x 11"; cut squares twice diagonally to yield 20 side triangles.
- ◎ 2 squares, 7" x 7"; cut squares once diagonally to yield 4 corner triangles.

From the assorted Japanese indigo prints for side A blocks, cut:
- ◎ 15 squares, each 7⅜" x 7⅜"; cut squares once diagonally to yield 30 large triangles.

From the assorted Indonesian batiks for side A blocks, cut:

- 15 squares, each 7⅜" x 7⅜"; cut squares once diagonally to yield 30 large triangles.

From the assorted tone-on-tone beige prints for side A blocks, cut:

- 29 squares, 7⅜" x 7⅜"; cut squares once diagonally to yield 58 large triangles.
- 5 squares, 11" x 11"; cut squares twice diagonally to yield 20 side triangles.
- 2 squares, 7" x 7"; cut squares once diagonally to yield 4 corner triangles.

From red print for side B, cut:

- 29 squares, 7" x 7", for plain blocks

From the assorted red prints for side B strips, cut:

- Narrow, medium, and wide strips as needed

From the black solid for side B, cut:

- 5 squares, 11" x 11"; cut squares twice diagonally to yield 20 side triangles.
- 2 squares, 7" x 7"; cut squares once diagonally to yield 4 corner triangles.

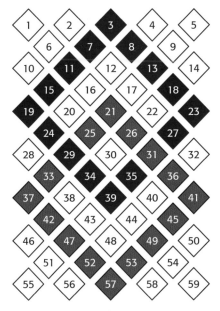

Side A

Directions

1. Make a colored sketch for each side. Starting in the upper left for side A and the upper right for side B, number the blocks from 1 to 59.

2. Referring to your colored sketch, "Block Variation 1," "Block Variation 2," and "Block Variation 4" on pages 19–20, make 59 blocks. Trim the blocks to 6½" x 6½".

3. Referring to your color sketch and the diagram at right (top), arrange the blocks for side A in diagonal rows. Referring to "Block Arrangement" on pages 24–25, turn the blocks over to view the blocks on side B **(fig. A)**.

4. Place a batting triangle between a black and a beige-print triangle. Pin or spray-baste; quilt as desired. See the tip box on page 62 for hints on quilting straight lines. Repeat for all side and corner triangles.

Side B

Fig. A

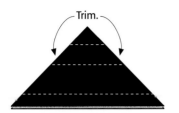

Trim.

Side setting triangle

Fig. B

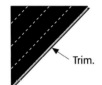

Trim.

Corner setting triangle

Fig. C

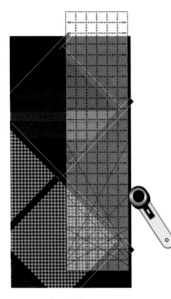

Trim 1" from
points of blocks.

Fig. D

5. Straighten the edges of the 2 short sides of the side triangles, trimming the minimum amount; leave the long side as is for now **(fig. B)**. Straighten the edge of the long side of the corner triangles, trimming the minimum amount; leave the 2 short sides as is for now **(fig. C)**.

6. Add the side and corner triangles to the diagonal rows.

7. Referring to "Basic Sashing: ⅝"-Wide" on pages 26–28, cut sashing strips for sides A and B. Join blocks and side triangles with sashing strips. Join the rows with sashing strips. To maintain the illusion of interlocking diamonds, you will need to piece the longer sashing strips (see "Pieced Sashing" on page 28). When you have 2 Japanese fabrics together, use a Japanese fabric for the sashing; when you have 2 Indonesian fabrics together, use an Indonesian fabric for the sashing. Whenever either one is sewn to a beige-print square, you can use any beige-print sashing strip.

8. To straighten the edges of the quilt, place the 1" mark of a long ruler on the points of the blocks and trim along the edge of the ruler with a rotary cutter **(fig. D)**.

9. Referring to "Basic Binding" or "Reversible Binding" on pages 34–38, bind the edges of the quilt.

Geese Behind Bars

Side A: Flying Geese

40½" x 44½"; 5 vertical rows of 4"- wide blocks; 2"-wide
sashing; 4"-wide border. INSET: **Side B:** Multicolor Bars

Side B: Multicolor Bars

W HEN MAKING A strippy pattern like this quilt, I find it's much easier to work with a pieced block on one side and a flexible pattern, such as bars, on the other side. Trying to match patterns with precise 1/4" seam allowances on both sides is difficult. So I like the freedom you get when you can trim one side to fit the other. The process for strippy quilts is simple. Sew the strips together first for each side; then layer the strips and quilt them before joining them with sashing and adding the borders. This is a great quilt in which to use fat eighths and fat quarters to get lots of variety in your fabrics.

Materials *42"-wide fabric*

- ◎ 3/4 yd. 96"-wide batting
- ◎ 3/4 yd. pink fabric for side A Flying Geese blocks
- ◎ 3/4 yd. total assorted prints for side A Flying Geese blocks
- ◎ 3/4 yd. print for side A border
- ◎ 1 1/4 yds. black solid for side B bars and border
- ◎ 2/3 yd. hand-dyed fabric for side B bars

For Wide Sashing
- ◎ 5/8 yd. for 2 1/2"-wide cut strips on side A
- ◎ 5/8 yd. for 2 1/2"-wide cut strips on side B

For Basic Binding
- ◎ 1/2 yd. for 2 1/2"-wide cut strips

For Reversible Binding
- ◎ 1/4 yd. for 1 1/8"-wide cut strips
- ◎ 1/3 yd. for 1 5/8"-wide cut strips

Cutting

From the batting, cut:
- ◎ 5 strips, 4 1/2" x 32 1/2", for vertical rows
- ◎ 2 strips, 5" x 29", for top and bottom border strips
- ◎ 2 strips, 5" x 46", for side border strips
- ◎ 4 strips, 1 1/4" x 32 1/2", for sashing
- ◎ 2 strips, 1 1/4" x 29", for sashing
- ◎ 2 strips, 1 1/4" x 46", for sashing

From the pink fabric for side A, cut:
- ◎ 160 squares, 2 1/2" x 2 1/2"

From the assorted prints for side A, cut:
- ◎ 80 rectangles, 2 1/2" x 4 1/2"

From the print for side A border, cut:
- ◎ 4 strips, 5" x 42", for borders
- ◎ 4 rectangles, 2 1/2" x 4 1/2", for border sashing pieces

From the sashing fabric for side A, cut:
- ◎ 8 strips, 2 1/2" x 42"

From the black solid for side B, cut:

- 3 strips, 4½" x 42", for bars; crosscut the strips into a variety of different-sized rectangles.
- 4 strips, 5" x 42", for border
- 4 rectangles, 2½" x 4½", for border sashing pieces
- 4 strips, 2½" x 42", for center sashing

From the hand-dyed fabric for side B, cut:

- 3 strips, 4½" x 42", for bars; crosscut the strips into a variety of different-sized rectangles.
- 4 strips, 2½" x 42", for sides, top and bottom sashing

Side A

1.   Draw a diagonal line on the wrong side of each 2½" square. See the tip box below for hints on using a paper guide. Place a 2½" square on one end of a 2½" x 4½" rectangle. Sew on the line, trim the seam allowance to ¼", and press the seam toward the triangle. Repeat with a second 2½" square at the other end of the rectangle. Make 80 units **(fig. A)**.

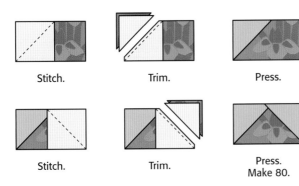

Stitch.   Trim.   Press.

Stitch.   Trim.   Press.
Make 80.

Fig. A

2.   Arrange and sew the Flying Geese blocks in vertical rows of 16 blocks each **(fig. B)**. The rows should be 32½" long. Make 5 rows.

32½"

Make 5.

Fig. B

To avoid drawing diagonal lines on the blocks, use a paper guide (see page 62). Align the corners of the block with the edge of the paper. Stitch along the edge of the paper.

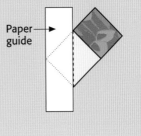

Paper guide

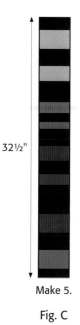

32½"

Make 5.

Fig. C

Side B

SEW THE BLACK and hand-dyed rectangles together in vertical rows, starting and ending with a black rectangle **(fig. C)**. Make 5 bar rows. Trim to 32½" to match the Flying Geese rows.

Assembling the Quilt Top

1.   Layer a Flying Geese row, a batting strip, and a bar row. Carefully pin or spray-baste. Because the Flying Geese were sewn to size, you won't be trimming very much later.

2.   With the Flying Geese blocks on top, quilt as desired. I quilted in the ditch around each unit with decorative thread in the bobbin and transparent nylon in the needle. If you quilt down one side and up the other, you can do it in one continuous line **(fig. D)**. Repeat for all vertical rows.

3.   Trim the rows to 4½" x 32½", being careful to leave the ¼"-wide seam allowances beyond the geese points. You should be trimming very little here; it's just a bit of tidying up.

4.   Referring to "Wide Sashing" on page 30, join the vertical rows with sashing strips.

5.   Join the strips for the side A border end to end to make one long strip. Cut 2 pieces, 5" x 46", for the side border strips, and 2 pieces, 5" x 29", for the top and bottom border strips. Repeat with the side B border strips.

6.   Place a batting strip between a side A and a side B border strip for the top and bottom. Pin or spray-baste, and quilt as desired. Make 2 border strips. Trim to 4½" x 28½".

7.   Place a piece of batting between a side A and a side B border strip for the sides. Pin or spray-baste, and quilt as desired. Make 2 border strips. Trim to 4½" x 44½".

Start here.

Quilt in the ditch
down one side
and up the other.

Fig. D

8. Referring to "Borders with a Contrasting Inner Border" on page 33, join the top and bottom border strips to the quilt with contrasting sashing strips. Referring to "Pieced Sashing" on page 28, sew a border fabric rectangle to each end of the sashing strips for the sides. Make 2 for each side of the quilt. Join the side borders to the quilt with the pieced sashing strips (fig. E).

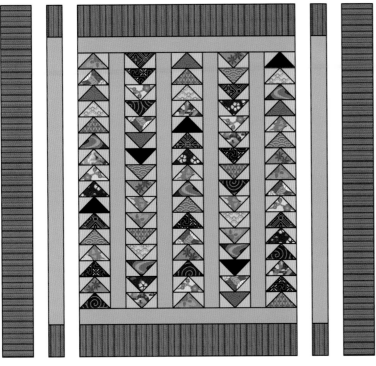

Fig. E

9. Referring to "Basic Binding" or "Reversible Binding" on pages 34–38, bind the edges of the quilt.

Wild & Woolly

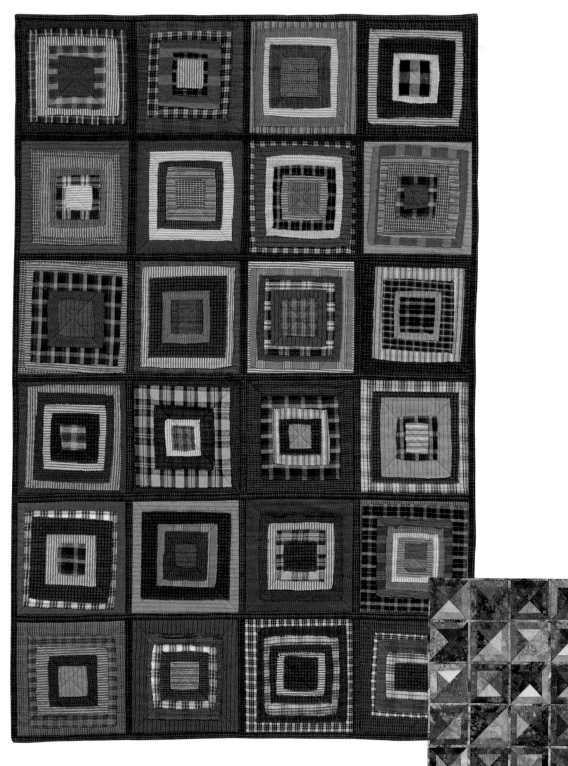

Side A: Flannel

38½" x 55⅝"; twenty-four 9" blocks set 4 across and 6 down;
⅝"-wide sashing. INSET: **Side B:** Batiks

Materials *42"-wide fabric*

- 1 yd. 96"-wide batting
- 3½ yds. total assorted flannels for side A
- 1⅝ yds. total assorted light batiks for side B triangles and frames
- 1⅝ yds. total assorted dark batiks for side B triangles and frames

For Basic ⅝"-Wide Sashing
- ⅜ yd. for 1⅛"-wide cut strips
- ⅝ yd. for 1¾"-wide cut strips

For Basic Binding
- ½ yd. for 2½"-wide cut strips

For Reversible Binding
- ¼ yd. for 1⅛"-wide cut strips
- ⅓ yd. for 1⅝"-wide cut strips

Cutting

From the batting, cut:
- 24 squares, 10" x 10"

From the assorted flannels for side A, cut:
- 24 squares, 10" x 10", for first square of block
- Assorted-sized squares for blocks (use pinking shears; see directions for side A below)

From the assorted light batiks for side B, cut:
- 12 squares, 7¼" x 7¼"; cut squares twice diagonally to yield 48 triangles.
- 48 strips, 2" x 12"; you will need 2 matching strips for each block.

From the assorted dark batiks for side B, cut:
- 12 squares, 7¼" x 7¼"; cut squares twice diagonally to yield 48 triangles.
- 48 strips, 2" x 12"; you will need 2 matching strips for each block.

Side B: Batiks

THIS QUILT WENT together quickly and was lots of fun to make. My friend Lynn McKitrick came over to help select fabrics for the batik side. Batiks are fun to work with because they have just enough surface design to make them interesting, but not so much that they make the quilt too busy. I used forty different batiks in this quilt, but you don't have to use that many to achieve wonderful results. In addition to the batiks, I also used a wonderful selection of hand-dyed fabrics that spanned the color wheel. For sashing, I found a batik that had all the colors from the quilt except fuchsia. I reasoned that there was enough fuchsia already in the quilt that it wouldn't appear to be an omission.

The flannel side has an equal number of fabrics—an accident I can assure you. Again, you could achieve wonderful results with fewer fabrics.

Providing yardage requirements is difficult for both sides of this quilt. On side A, each square produces a smaller square that is cut out after the stitching is done. The largest square in each block is the only square cut with a ruler and rotary cutter; all the others are cut freehand with pinking shears and are therefore only approximations. This is a great quilt in which to use a variety of fat quarters.

Fig. A

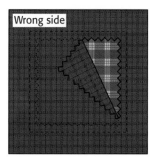

Fig. B

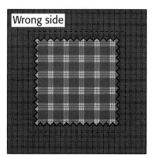

Fig. C

Save for another block.

Fig. D

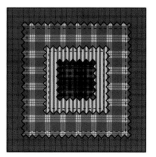

Fig. E

Side A

THE FIRST SQUARE for each block is the only one cut with a rotary cutter; cut all other squares with pinking shears. If you are making a scrap quilt, cut one square at a time so you can make design decisions as your quilt takes shape on the design wall.

1.   On the right side of a 10" flannel square, place a smaller square cut with pinking shears from another fabric, right side up. How much smaller is up to you. With transparent nylon in the needle and a neutral-colored thread in the bobbin, sew the smaller square to the larger one approximately ¼" from the pinked edge **(fig. A)**.

2.   Turn the block over, and with sharp-pointed scissors, cut an opening ¼" from the stitching line, making a slit big enough for the point of the pinking shears **(fig. B)**.

3.   With pinking shears, trim all around the square, leaving a ¼"-wide seam allowance **(fig. C)**. The piece you trim off the back can be used on the front of another block **(fig. D)**.

4.   Continue putting a smaller block on top of the previous one, sewing and trimming until you are pleased with the block **(fig. E)**. The number of fabrics on my squares varies from 5 to 7. I think it is more interesting if you vary the fabric width that shows from block to block as well.

5.   On your design wall, arrange the blocks in 6 vertical rows of 4 blocks each. Starting in the upper left-hand corner, number the blocks from 1–24.

6.   Remove the blocks, keeping them in order.

Side B

1.   Arrange 2 light triangles and 2 dark triangles as shown. Place 2 matching light strips next to the light triangles, and 2 matching dark strips next to the dark triangles **(fig. F)**. The 2 light strips should not match the triangles, but they should match each other; the same goes for the dark strips.

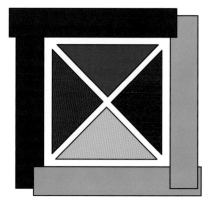

Fig. F

2. Center the long edge of a triangle on the edge of a strip. Sew the triangle to the strip with a ¼"-wide seam allowance **(fig. G)**.

3. Press the seams as shown so that the seams will butt together when the triangles are joined **(fig. H)**. Place the corner of a square ruler (or triangular ruler) on the point of the triangle and even with the sides. Trim both sides of the strip **(fig. I)**. Repeat for all triangles.

4. Matching seams carefully, join 2 light triangle segments. Do the same with 2 dark triangle segments. Press the seams in opposite directions. Do not sew the light side to the dark side. Repeat for all triangle segments.

5. Arrange the light and dark triangle segments on a design wall and number the blocks from 1–24, starting in the upper right corner. Remember this is the reverse of side A.

Assembling the Quilt Top

1. Working on one block at a time, place block 1 from side A face down on your work surface, and cover with a batting square **(fig. J)**. Pin 2 triangles for block 1 from side B to the batting square.

2. Put the walking foot on your machine.

3. With transparent nylon thread in your bobbin and a neutral-colored thread in the needle, stitch through all the layers. Open the triangle and finger-press.

4. Quilt in the ditch along the other diagonal seam.

5. Trim the blocks to 9½" x 9½". There should be 1 diagonal on your ruler. To make the job easier, add a second diagonal to your ruler with masking tape, or draw 2 diagonals on a 9½" x 9½" piece of acrylic.

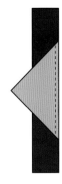

Fig. G

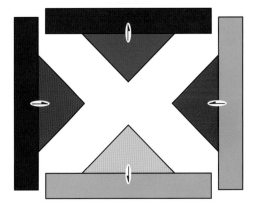

Fig. H

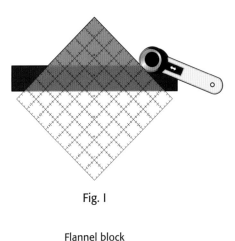

Fig. I

Flannel block underneath

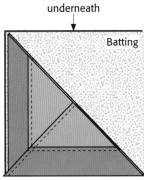

Batting

Side B

Fig. J

NOTE: *If your square ruler is larger than 9½", for the second diagonal, place a piece of masking tape along a diagonal line from the 9½" mark on one side to the 9½" mark on the other side.*

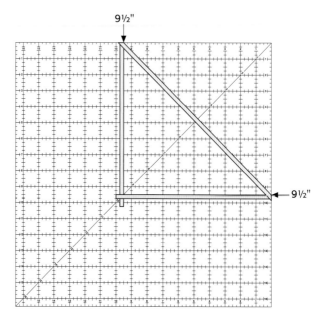

Center the diagonal lines on the ruler with the diagonal stitching lines of the block. Trim the side and top edges. Then turn the block around, center the diagonal lines again, and trim the remaining two edges of the block. The first two edges you trimmed should be at the 9½" lines on the ruler.

6. Referring to "Basic Sashing: ⅝"-Wide" on pages 26–28, cut sashing strips for sides A and B. Join the blocks and rows with sashing strips.

7. Referring to "Basic Binding" or "Reversible Binding" on pages 34–38, bind the edges of the quilt.

The Eleventh Hour

Side A: Black and White Prints
28" x 28"; twenty-five 5" blocks set 5 across and 5 down;
⅝"-wide sashing. INSET: **Side B:** Batiks and Hand-Dyed Fabrics

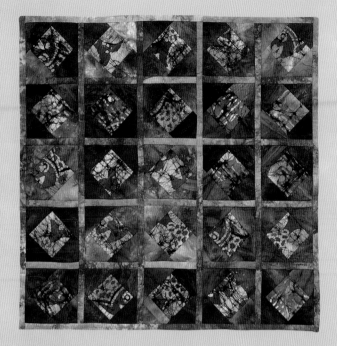

Side B: Batiks and Hand-Dyed Fabrics

D o you sometimes wonder why quilts are given the names they have? It's safe to admit, now that the crisis is over, why this one is called "The Eleventh Hour." While I was in the final stages of preparing the manuscript for this book, I realized that I had counted one quilt twice. How can that happen, you ask? I had included one quilt in two categories in the proposed list of projects and discovered rather late in the game that I had only nine quilts made, not the ten I needed. Fortunately, I had a set of blocks made for another project, and my friend Lynn McKitrick rescued me by agreeing to sew the second side.

This is another great project in which to use fat eighths or fat quarters so you can get a greater variety of fabrics.

Materials *42"-wide fabric*

- ⊚ ⅜ yd. 96"-wide batting
- ⊚ ½ yd. total assorted white-with-black prints (lights) for side A
- ⊚ ½ yd. total assorted black-with-white prints (darks) for side A
- ⊚ ⅜ yd. multicolor batik for side B center squares
- ⊚ 1⅛ yds. hand-dyed fabric for side B corner triangles

For Basic ⅝"-Wide Sashing
- ⊚ ¼ yd. for 1⅛"-wide cut strips
- ⊚ ⅜ yd. for 1¾"-wide cut strips

For Basic Binding
- ⊚ ¼ yd. for 2½"-wide cut strips

For Reversible Binding
- ⊚ ⅛ yd. for 1⅛"-wide cut strips
- ⊚ ¼ yd. for 1⅝"-wide cut strips

Cutting

From the batting, cut:
- ⊚ 25 squares, 6" x 6"

From the assorted white-with-black prints (lights) for side A, cut:
- ⊚ 13 squares, 3½" x 3½", for center squares
- ⊚ 12 strips, 1¾" x 20", for frame around squares

From the assorted black-with-white prints (darks) for side A, cut:
- ⊚ 12 squares, 3½" x 3½", for center squares
- ⊚ 13 strips, 1¾" x 20", for frame around squares

From the multicolor batik for side B, cut:

◎ 25 squares, 3½" x 3½", for center squares

From the hand-dyed fabric for side B, cut:

◎ 25 squares, 7" x 7"; cut squares twice diagonally to yield
100 triangles

Fig. A

Side A

1.   Sew a 1¾"-wide dark black-with-white strip to opposite sides of a 3½" light white-with-black square **(fig. A)**. You can cut the strips to 3½" before sewing, or use the full strip length and trim the sides after sewing.

2.   Sew a matching 1¾"-wide dark strip to the remaining sides of the square and trim **(fig. B)**. Make 13 squares with light white-with-black centers surrounded by dark black-with-white strips.

3.   Repeat steps 1 and 2 to make 12 squares with dark black-with-white centers surrounded by light white-with-black strips **(fig. C)**.

4.   Referring to the color photo on page 77, arrange the blocks for side A, alternating light and dark center squares. Number the blocks in horizontal rows from 1 to 25, starting in the top left corner.

Make 13
with light centers.

Fig. B

Side B

1.   Find the center of the side A blocks and the batik squares by folding each of them in half horizontally and vertically. Finger-press the center creases in both directions. Matching the center points, place a side A block, right side down, on your work surface; then add a batting square, and a batik square on point **(fig. D)**. Stick a pin through all 3 layers to be sure the centers match.

2.   With right sides together, place the long edge of a triangle on the side of the on-point square, centering the point of the triangle with the middle of the square. With neutral-colored thread in the needle and transparent nylon in the bobbin, sew the triangle along the long edge from one edge of the batting square to the other. Repeat with a triangle on the opposite side of the square. Open the triangles and finger-press **(fig. E)**.

Make 12
with dark centers.

Fig. C

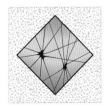

Fig. D

Black-with-white
block underneath

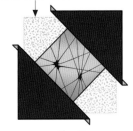

Fig. E

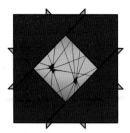

Fig. F

3. Sew 2 triangles to the remaining corners. Open triangles and finger-press **(fig. F)**.

NOTE: *Stitching the triangles to the square results in quilted lines on side A, so there is no need to do any additional quilting unless you desire to do so.*

Assembling the Quilt Top

1. Working from side A, trim the block to 5½" x 5½". I used my 5½" clear acrylic square with 2 diagonals drawn on it. If you're using a standard square ruler, add a second diagonal with ¼"-wide masking tape. Center the diagonals on the 4 corners of the center square and trim the side and top edges. Then turn the block around, center the diagonal lines again, and trim the remaining 2 edges of the block **(fig. G)**.

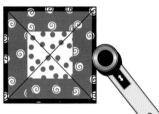

Fig. G

2. Return the blocks for side A to your design wall. Referring to "Block Arrangement" on pages 24–25, turn the blocks over to view the blocks on side B.

3. Referring to "Basic Sashing: ⅝"-Wide" on pages 26–28, cut sashing strips for sides A and B. Join the blocks and rows with sashing strips.

4. Referring to "Basic Binding" or "Reversible Binding" on pages 34–38, bind the edges of the quilt.

I Spy a Rogue

Side A: Rogues Gallery
57" x 57"; twenty-five 9" blocks set 5 across and 5 down;
⅝"-wide sashing; 4½"-wide border. INSET: **Side B:** I Spy

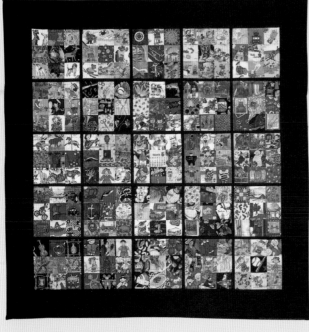

Side B: I Spy

For my first grandchild's fifth birthday, I decided to make an I Spy quilt. To supplement my collection of I Spy blocks, and just for fun, I held an "I Spy Swap Meet" for all of the grandmothers in my quilt group. There were six of us, and we spent the day cutting 3½" squares and trading them. I used 260 squares in Haley's quilt and still had over a hundred left. Over the course of the next year, I added another 150 squares to my collection, in anticipation of another grandchild.

When Haley's little brother was born, I started thinking about how to make a quilt for Finlay that was a little different. I immediately thought about photo transfers for one side. Then he could play "I Spy" or "Name That Relative."

My plan was to make Nine Patch blocks for the I Spy side and photo blocks for the other. The problem was the size of the I Spy blocks. Because I used 3½" cut squares, the finished blocks were 9". But the photos could only be 8" square because of the size of the transfer paper. Consequently, I decided to leave a ½" border of white around each photo group. If I hadn't already collected over 250 I Spy blocks, each 3½", I would have cut them 4½" and made Four Patch blocks for the I Spy side.

Materials *42"-wide fabric*

- 1⅜ yds. 96"-wide batting
- 2¼ yds. white solid suitable for side A photo blocks
- ½ yd. black solid for side A corners and for lining small photos
- 1 yd. dark gray print for side A borders
- 225 novelty print squares*, 3½" x 3½", for I Spy blocks on side B
- 1 yd. black solid for side B borders
- Photographs and 8½" x 11" photo-transfer sheets (as many as needed for photos)

For Basic ⅝"-Wide Sashing
- ⅝ yd. for 1⅛"-wide cut strips
- ⅞ yd. for 1¾"-wide cut strips

For Basic Binding
- ½ yd. for 2½"-wide cut strips

For Reversible Binding
- ¼ yd. for 1⅛"-wide cut strips
- ⅜ yd. for 1⅝"-wide cut strips

*To cut the squares, use a 3½" acrylic square or make a window template from cardboard. See "Resources" on page 94 for information about acrylic squares. Place ¼"-wide masking tape around the edge of the 3½" acrylic square. This allows you to see what the image will look like when it is sewn into a block. The best part of using the acrylic square is that you can zip around the square with your rotary cutter.

Making Photo Transfers

GATHER THE PHOTOGRAPHS and arrange them in groups so that they can be photocopied onto 8½" x 11" photo-transfer paper. (See "Resources" on page 94 for ordering Photo Transfer Paper from Martingale & Company.) Reduce or enlarge photos as needed to fit an 8" x 8" area. The number of pictures in each group varies from one to five. If you want to make different-size blocks, determine the size for the photo area and reduce or enlarge photos as needed to fill the space.

It's a good idea to buy more than you actually need. I guarantee that there will be some glitches. In my case, the person doing the photocopying forgot to mirror-image the pictures, so some of my relatives became left-handed.

Following the manufacturer's instructions, I tried to do the transferring at home but found that a household iron isn't good enough, particularly if you are doing images that are larger than the base of your iron. I tried a few, with two different irons, and wasn't happy with the results.

So off I went in search of a heat press. Some quilt shops have a heat press that you can use for a fee. I ended up at a company that makes custom-designed T-shirts. They had a wonderful heat press that applied even pressure across the whole sheet, plus it had a timer and a thermostat. To achieve the best results, peel the backing paper off while the fabric is still hot. To do this, we left the fabric on the heat press and peeled the backing off while it was kept hot. This is definitely a January project, not one for July.

To make a window template from cardboard, cut a 3½" square from thin cardboard. Draw a line ¼" from the edge all around **(fig. A)**. Carefully cut out the inside square. The inside measurement is the finished size of the square. Use the window template to isolate suitable images on the fabric **(fig. B)**. Draw around the outside edge of the template with a pencil, and cut out the square with scissors.

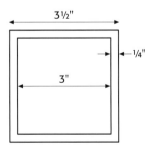

Fig. A

Fig. B

Cutting

From the batting, cut:
- 25 squares, 10" x 10"
- 2 strips, 5½" x 49", for top and bottom border strips
- 2 strips, 5½" x 58", for side border strips

From the white solid for side A, cut:
- 25 squares, 10" x 10"

From the black solid for side A, cut:
- 100 squares, 2¼" x 2¼", for corners
- 16 squares, 2½" x 2½", for lining small photos

From the dark gray print for side A borders, cut:
- 6 strips, 5½" x 42"

From the black solid for side B borders, cut:
- 6 strips, 5½" x 42"

Side A

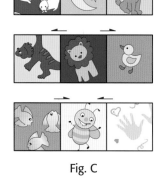

Fig. C

1.   Referring to the manufacturer's directions, transfer your photos to the 10" white solid squares, centering the images within the square as much as possible (see "Making Photo Transfers" on page 83).

2.   Arrange the photos on your design wall. Number the blocks in horizontal rows from 1 to 25, starting in the top left corner.

3.   Remove the blocks, keeping them in order.

Side B

1.   Arrange the novelty print squares on your design wall in groups of 9 squares, 3 across and 3 down. Join the 9 squares in horizontal rows first **(fig. C)**; then join the rows to complete the block **(fig. D)**. Make 25 I Spy blocks.

2.   Arrange the I Spy blocks on your design wall. Number the blocks in horizontal rows from 1 to 25, starting in the top right corner; the opposite corner from which you started numbering the blocks on side A. Remember, side B is the reverse of side A.

Make 25.

Fig. D

Assembling the Quilt Top

1. Working on block 1 from side A and block 1 from side B, center the I Spy block on top of a batting square and a photo block. The photo block is ½" larger to allow for some slippage while you quilt. Pin or spray-baste, and quilt as desired. From the photo block side, I quilted around each photograph with black thread in the needle and transparent nylon thread in the bobbin. This helped to separate the photos visually from one another in the block.

2. From the photo block side, trim the blocks to 9½" x 9½". Use a square ruler with the diagonals marked on it. Align the diagonal lines with the corners of the photo square. Remember, the I Spy block is already 9½", so there's very little that has to be trimmed.

3. Draw a diagonal line on the wrong side of the 2¼" black squares, or use a paper guide (see the tip box on page 62). Place a square on a corner of the block as shown and sew on the diagonal line. Trim the excess black fabric ¼" beyond the seam line; do not trim the corner of the photo block or the batting **(fig. E)**. Press the triangle toward the corner, being careful not to touch the photos with the iron **(fig. F)**. Repeat for the remaining corners.

Fig. E

4. As you trim the blocks, return them to their original position on your design wall.

5. Referring to "Basic Sashing: ⅝"-Wide" on pages 26–28, cut the sashing strips for sides A and B. Join the blocks and then the rows with sashing strips.

6. Join the border pieces for side A end to end to make 1 long strip. Cut 2 pieces, each 49" long, for the top and bottom border strips, and 2 pieces, each 58" long, for the side border strips. Repeat with the border strips for side B.

Fig. F

7. Place a piece of batting between a side A border strip and a side B border strip. Pin or spray-baste, and quilt as desired. Make 4 border strips. Trim the top and bottom border strips to 5" x 48", and the side border strips to 5" x 57".

8. Referring to "Basic Borders" on page 32, join the top and bottom border strips to the quilt with sashing strips. Join the side border strips to the quilt with sashing strips.

Leave open
for turning.

Fig. G

Fig. H

9. Referring to "Basic Binding" or "Reversible Binding" on pages 34–38, bind the edges of the quilt.

OPTIONAL: *If you want to cover the black diamonds created by the triangles on the photo blocks, you can appliqué a small photo on each diamond. The photos will be placed on point, so you need to select 16 small photos that will fit into an on-point square that finishes to 2" x 2". Transfer the photos to white fabric. Leaving ¼" around the photo for seam allowances, cut the fabric 2½" x 2½". With right sides together, sew a 2½" black square to a photo square, leaving an opening for turning (**fig. G**). Turn the photo right side out and finger-press.*

Center the small photo on the black diamond at the intersections; appliqué the photos by hand or machine (**fig. H**).

THE REVERSIBLE QUILT technique has opened up many design doors for me—more than I can show in the "Projects" section of the book. The following examples are a few more by me, and some from my very talented friends.

Rae's Stars

by Sharon Pederson, 40" x 40". I made this quilt in memory of my dad, Rae Jones, using the wonderful patterns of Hari Walner (see "Resources" on page 94).

Touched by Japan

by Sharon Pederson, 32½" x 36½".
I killed three birds with one stone
with this quilt. It works as a sample
for three classes I teach: Japanese
Family Crests, Sashiko by Machine,
and Reversible Quilts.

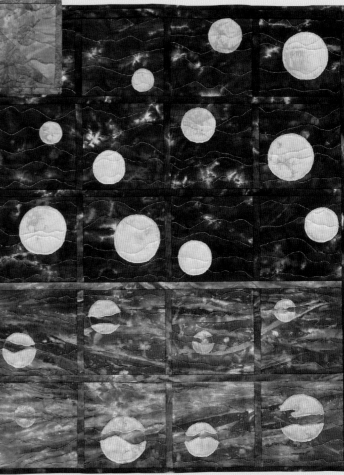

Sunrises/Moonrises

by Ionne McCauley, 28" x 35".
Sunrise over the sea and moonlight on the water—Ionne used her own hand-dyed fabrics to make the circles on the sunrise side appear transparent.

Boomers Reach 50

Drawings by Judie Hansen, quilt made by Sharon Pederson, 44¾" x 22½". My friend Judie Hansen is a great cartoonist. I asked her for some drawings of women "of a certain age," and she provided me with this delightful quartet. I had too much fun making this quilt. It makes me smile every time I see it.

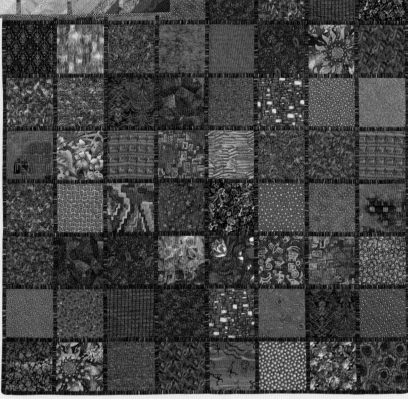

Playing in My Paintbox

by Pippa Moore, 60" x 70".
Like most quilters, Pippa enjoys
nothing more than spending time
playing with her fabrics and
imagining possible ways to combine
them in a quilt. "Playing in My
Paintbox" resulted from just such a
time with a rainbow run of fabrics.

Reversible Quilt

by Maurine Roy, 82" x 92½".
Maurine is every teacher's dream
student. She takes a technique and
runs with it. Not only did she create
a unique and beautiful design, but
she did it entirely by machine.

A Quilt for Kathy Nilsson

by Paulette Galloway, 66" x 66".
Designing this star presented
Paulette with a few interesting
challenges—including integrating
the connecting ribs as a design
element.

Patterns by Hari Walner

> Beautiful Publications
> 7508 Paul Place
> Loveland, CO 80537-8732
> Phone: 970-622-9950
> Fax: 970-461-0599
> quilting@earthlink.net

Continuous-line machine-quilting patterns from the Designer Collection and the Bouquet Collection were used as appliqué patterns in "Rae's Stars" on page 87.

Japanese Design Motifs: 4260 Illustrations of Japanese Crests

> Compiled by the Matsuya Piece-Goods Store
> Dover Publications
> ISBN: 0-486-22874-6

Patterns used in "Touched by Japan" on page 88.

Clear Acrylic Squares *(sometimes referred to as Plexiglas, Lucite, Perspex, or Acrylite, which are all registered brand names)*

To buy the clear acrylic squares seen on page 8, refer to your yellow pages for "Plastics—Fabricating." Any company that makes clear plastic bins for bulk food sales or similar items should be able to cut squares of clear acrylic for you in any size. The thickness you want is ⅛". The price in Canada is $3.79 a square foot, but often you can find very inexpensive pieces in a company's scrap bin.

Photo Transfer Paper

> Martingale & Company
> 20205 144th Avenue NE
> Woodinville, WA 98072
> Phone: 800-426-3126
> www.martingale-pub.com

SHARON PEDERSON was born and raised in Vancouver, British Columbia. She learned to sew from her mother when she was very young. In fact, Sharon was so young that she could not reach the treadle of the sewing machine while sitting on the seat. To sew, she would stand on one leg and treadle with the other. Her mother insists she had no choice in the matter; Sharon was determined to sew—right then!

Sharon married young and had two wonderful daughters, Gail and Heather. Then she grew up and divorced. For many years, she worked as a political organizer, traveling from coast to coast in Canada.

The year 1986 was a big one for Sharon—she remarried and discovered quilting. When she started to teach quilting, Sharon realized that she preferred the creative world of quilting to political organizing, so she gave up politics to become a full-time quilting teacher.

In 1996 Sharon was on the road again after she took a job as a sales rep for a wholesale fabric distributor. She also continued to teach and was hardly ever home. After four years of selling fabric to quilt shops, Sharon retired with a house full of swatches and returned to her first loves: making quilts and teaching.

When not traveling to teach, Sharon is living happily ever after in a small house filled with quilts and fabric, her wonderful, supportive husband, and a very neurotic cat.

You can visit Sharon at www.sharonquilts.com.